D0967935

Calling Angel One

Calling Angel One

Bob Turnbull

Published by Bible Voice Books
P. O. Box 7491
Van Nuys, Calif. 91409

Following versions of the Bible have been quoted in this book:

King James Version (KJV).

The New American Standard Bible (NASB). The Lockman Foundation, La Habra, California, 1971.

The Living Bible, Paraphrased (TLB). Tyndale House Publishers, Wheaton, Illinois, 1971.

 Printed in U.S.A. Published by Bible Voice, Inc. P.O. Box 7491 Van Nuys, CA 91409.

DEDICATED TO

Our Lord Jesus Christ; and

All police chiefs everywhere, especially Chief Keala (Honolulu), Chief White (Palm Springs) and Chief Davis (Los Angeles); and

All the men and women who are members of "The Thin Blue Line"; and

Finally, to my son, Kekoakalani

INTRODUCTION

I would like to share a couple of thoughts with you as you prepare to read this book:

I was perplexed as I thought about what to title this book. At least a hundred titles could be used and all of them quite suitable. I finally settled on "Calling Angel One." That was my code name during my duty with the Palm Springs Police Department.

Angel means messenger of God and that's what police chaplains, and this book, are all about. It is about messengers of God to police personnel and often to the public as well.

It would have been impossible to list all the experiences I've had as a police chaplain. I've worked with the Honolulu Police Department, on a somewhat personal basis with Palm Springs, and with other police departments on a one-shot basis as I traveled the nation.

The experiences and stories depicted in this book are sometimes several incidents condensed into one. This journalistic license allowed me to make a succinct presentation in print. Actual sequential narration would require a 1200-page journal.

May this book be a positive influence in your community, a catalyst in presenting answers and may it strengthen your resolve in being truly free.

Mahalo nui loa (thank you very much).

Bob Turnbull

TABLE OF CONTENTS

FOREWORD

Can Jesus enter the lives of prostitutes, pushers, and pimps? Can He touch burglars, hold-up men and looters? Can He halt homosexual hassles and domestic squabbles and tempers? Can He make life easier for police thrust into the cauldron of man's inhumanity to man?

I know He can.

I'm a "Police Chaplain."

The chaplain is an integral part of virtually every military organization chart. Yet relatively few police departments have chaplains. Those that do find they have a unique weapon in the fight against crime.

Are you a police chief, a town official, a taxpayer? Then come with me for a typical night cruise in a police car, for a conversation with a policeman who "wants out," for a visit to the emergency ward, for a ride in the wagon with a prostitute, for an on-the-spot confrontation with an armed robber.

You will know then, as I do, how singularly well the clerical collar and police badge go together. You will push for the spirit of the Lord to enter police work in your community.

Shall we take off? We may have a 519 call—an auto accident; an 800—berserk person; an 802—death; a 410—family fight. But we'll have help—Jesus will be riding with us.

CHAPTER ONE

A Typical Night For The Police Chaplain

It was busy in the police locker room. The day watch was wrapping it up. The night watch was just coming on.

I was getting it from both ends. "Rough out there today, Bob. Better bring along an extra Bible." "Hey, Chaplain Bob. I'm transferred to Waimanalo. Pray for me."

Earlier that day I had called personnel at police headquarters.

"I'll be cruising tonight."

I liked to get down so I could see the fellows in both watches—shake hands, swap stories and rap.

A police officer slung his uniform into the locker, tossing it in like a towel.

"How'd it go, Tom?" I asked.

He let go with a few choice four-letter words.

"I get no respect," I replied lightly.

"You don't have your collar on yet."

He was right. I was just getting into my uniform, which was a black and white clerical collar, aloha shirt (bush-jacket style), black pants and shoes, and my badge. Below it was my name on an ID card.

"Who's the dude just came in?" I nodded my head in the direction of a young man I had not seen before.

"A recruit. Introduce yourself."

I did. "I'm Chaplain Bob Turnbull. You going out on this watch?"

"Yeah. My name's Kawakami. Tim Kawakami. I was just reading the board. See where there's an escapee movin' around."

"Right," I said grimly. "Oahu prison. He'll probably head for Waikiki where I'll be tonight."

"Me, too." The rookie's hand had moved unconsciously toward the holster he was wearing.

I had reached automatically for my card. "If I can ever be of assistance to you." He took it with a nod.

It was time for the briefing and we filed into the room. The commander came in, and laid his words out: "Facts for tonight." Notebooks snapped open. "We have our friend Sam, the Gun, on the loose again. He's armed and dangerous. Might be in the Waikiki area. Be careful. Go in twos. You guys in that area, especially near the Jungle, be sure you have a back-up unit on standby within a few blocks. We've brought in men from other areas so we'll be saturating the Jungle.

"Be especially alert. There's been a rash of purse snatching along the Ala Wai Canal. Probably some kids in from the country. It may have just been a one night hit, but be alert anyhow. Warn women carrying bags to use the kind with shoulder straps.

"The Perkins family on Kailani Street is at it again. You guys get ready for a domestic. I see our police chaplain, Bob Turnbull, is here. Chaplain, hang loose. We may call you in on this one.

"This is pay-day weekend. Always a bad one for us. They'll be hitting the Primo beer. That's about it, men."

I got my kit of supplies—I always had these with me—a blanket, flashlight, Mace, flares, and diary. Then I checked out the car. The condition of the police car, before and after each watch, had to be recorded and a full report turned in. This meant jotting down any dents or damages.

This night I was cruising in my own car. Next time I might be riding along with another officer in his. I picked up the radio phone and gave my chaplain's code: "Angel One." I had a number also (1492), but I preferred giving this code.

"Come in, Angel One," replied the dispatcher.

"This is Police Chaplain Turnbull. I'm in Waikiki sector tonight. Cruising and available."

"Ten four," she acknowledged.

Now all the other cars heard on their radios that I was available—the officers I missed at the change of watch or those who were doing overtime or double duty. Central had a file card that the chaplain was on the road and "available," and so . . . I was ready for "business."

The radio continued to gargle out all the rapid chatter, mostly in numbered codes that indicated suspected prowlers, robbers, blocked driveways. I don't respond to those unless requested.

Several years ago when Honolulu's Dan Liu founded the first police chaplaincy in Hawaii, calls on the radio were few and far between. Now there is a constant chatter, unintelligible to the untrained ears. Mine are able not only to understand but to tuck away the information for possible use later in that watch. I may get a call from an officer involving one of these calls. He may need some help. That is my first responsibility—to help a fellow officer. There is a responsibility to the public, too, but the welfare of the police force gets priority.

My ears were especially tuned in for calls about car wrecks, or domestic squabbles, or crowd control situations. I responded to those calls without being given a special radioed invitation.

"A rear-ender. Corner Kalakaua and Kapahulu. Occupant injured. Ambulance en route."

That meant me. I swung around and turned up Kalakaua. Waiting for an ambulance is a problem time for an officer. I stepped on the gas pedal, but no flashing lights, no siren. In about 45 seconds I was there. As I pulled up, I quickly surveyed the situation—if the officer had it under control, I'd go on. No use my getting bogged down and kept from some other area where I was needed more. I try not to get involved where I am not really needed.

In this case I saw the need. A woman had taken her eyes off the road to look at the ocean and rammed a van that had stopped suddenly for pedestrians. She was bleeding profusely. Her child on the front seat with her was screaming hysterically.

Only one officer had arrived and was trying to get things sorted out. I immediately went over to calm the ten-year-old girl, picked her up in my arms and held her so she would not see the blood still oozing from her mother.

"Your mother will feel better if you stop crying," I told her. "She is going to be all right. What's your name?"

Her screaming turned into convulsive sobs. The officer gave me a look of thanks, freed as he was now to clear the street, guide traffic, call the towing company, the whole bit.

I sat down on the grass with the little girl clinging to me and still sobbing. Another patrolman arrived on foot and was tending the mother. When the ambulance arrived, I took the little girl in my car and we followed it to the hospital. I stayed long enough to see the two reunited and a doctor's report that the mother's injuries were only superficial.

Back once more cruising in Waikiki, the radio talk continued incessantly, its note of urgency diminishing as the nerves adjusted. I passed a construction site—some youths were hanging around a pile of materials. My turn to add to the rasping radio: I suggested a look-see by any nearby patrol car.

The watch commander was right. A call about a domestic quarrel identified that same Perkins family on Kailani Street. "Here is where this Jesus Cop gets a call," I thought. I was only a few blocks away.

I cruised around the area. Ten minutes later a plaintive

voice came over the radio. I immediately recognized it as that of the rookie cop I had just met. He was putting a "help wanted" ad on the air.

"Is the police chaplain available?"

I answered him directly instead of going through Central.

"Ten four. I hear you. Where is your location?"

He confirmed the Kailani Street address.

"On the way."

"Ten four."

When I arrived, he was already back in the apartment. Neighbors were standing around the street, in the hallways, and outside the apartment door. You could hear the couple yelling a block away.

I walked into the dimly lit room as a beer can came hurtling by. The guy had thrown it at his wife and had another in his hand ready to go. He froze. I saw the light from the hallway reflected on the can, and it must have reflected on my collar, too, then. He dropped the beer can and fell on his knees.

"Father, forgive me, forgive me."

It was an extreme case of a domestic quarrel. It was an even more extreme response to the arrival of a police chaplain. He saw a Roman Catholic collar. He was Roman Catholic. Previously, the rookie cop's presence had only served to rile him up, and he was ready to take on his wife and him both.

The wife was standing ready to duck the next object. When she saw her husband fall to his knees, she said, "What the hell are you . . . ?" Then she turned and saw me. I didn't affect her that much, but the effect I had on him stopped her short.

I figured I'd better take quick advantage of this and pull a Cecil B. de Mille move. I'd appeared before him out of thin air—now I walked up to him. "My son, arise and sit down and speak not," I said with King James-like authority.

The wife sat down, too. For them both it was instant sobriety, based on fear.

Another person in the room sat down, too—the rookie cop. He never heard of a domestic fight like that in recruit class, nor had he ever seen a fight stop so precipitously. He gave an audible sigh of relief as he collapsed in a chair.

I did not have to talk very long. There was nothing to talk about. Their penance was so thick you could cut it. I just told them to go to bed. As I got in my car, their room lights went out.

Who am I? I know who I am in the eyes of the people in churches, on beaches and at meetings where I preach. I know who I am to the couples I marry, the people I bury, and the distressed souls I counsel.

But who am I to the police?

My thoughts go back a couple of weeks to the last recruit class I addressed. This was the hour reserved in their training when recruits meet the police chaplain. It is the first time they see such a creature, and many hear for the first time that one exists.

They have spent some twenty weeks drilling, going through physical training, and hearing people speak on rules and regulations: the constitutional aspects of law enforcement, department policy, the criminal justice system, the penal code, rules of evidence, and even child-birth procedures and cardio-pulmonary resuscitation.

It all makes sense. You cannot be a police officer unless you know how to search, arrest, defend yourself, shoot accurately, fingerprint, give traffic citations, recognize organized crime characters, handle sex offenders, and know courtroom procedures. But what has a chaplain got to do with all of this?

When I have introduced myself to these rookies, it helps to clarify my role for me, too. It's easy to get caught up in the nitty-gritty of keeping man's laws and forget about God's laws.

I walked into the class, and the way I do this was important—like writing Chapter One of a book. The first minute could set up for the rest of their lives their image of a police chaplain. El Weirdo or regular guy.

"Good morning, fifty-fourth recruits."

Their teachers have addressed them this way so far in their training. So they responded as they always have in unison, "Good morning, sir."

"My name is Bob Turnbull."

I continued quite business-like and in the clipped military manner that other police have spoken to them. "I'm one of the chaplains of the Honolulu Police Department. I'm here to explain the program to you. This won't be an hour of boredom. If you want to laugh, laugh. If you get mad, get mad. Let your emotions be real, because I promise to be real with you."

All eyes were front now.

"Those of you who listen to KKUA, and have heard *Soul Talk* know who I am."

That clicked with half the class. "Oh yeah," rippled around. They were all kids and had grown up listening to it for the last eight years.

"That's right. Brother Bob laying the chaplain sounds on you on the heavy program."

Laughter. Now the other half of the class was with me.

Then I followed with some of the police "war" stories that I will tell you on the pages ahead—my encounters with pimps and prostitutes, gamblers and gangsters. I spiced them up with some of my past experiences in Hollywood, and with my present experiences on the television show, "Hawaii Five-O."

I gave them a rundown of my duties as spelled out by the department regulations. My first duty toward the morale and spiritual well-being of the police officer—how that is implemented; my duties as an in-house pastor for hospital calls, home visits, weddings and funerals; and finally that gray area of responsibility having to do with ride-alongs, cruising, and lending assistance at the scene of whatever it is.

I spent some time on this latter part as I wanted them to know that their police chaplain would not be entering this area unless called upon by them.

"Part of my duty is to participate in recruit orientation. I am glad I am able to do this. Yes, I want you to know we are available for counseling. Yes, I want you to know we are available for community assistance. But most of all this hour has given you a chance to see me, so before you bust somebody in Waikiki make sure it's not me giving some crook a sermon!"

The moment of truth arrived and I do get spiritually serious.

"My life-style is marching with Jesus. You talk about a badge. He's got the best badge ever—pure gold and eternal. When He flashes it, I listen. He's not carrying a nightstick. He's not a cosmic cop who's going to lean on you. He's there to love you and support you and be part of your life forever—if you'll let Him!

"Some of you will have experience with the city morgue. You'll check out some bodies that are no longer alive. You'll read the stats. Check the tags. And see how they are put in the cooler. They are all very dead and some day, men, you'll be too.

"That's why you should have a positive answer for all your needs, not just for today but forever. And that's why I am here."

Was I qualified to be one of their police chaplains? I asked that question and then had them read with me the pertinent parts of the general police department order spelling these out:

1. An ordained minister, priest or individual licensed by a duly-recognized religious body compatible to, and in conformance with, the religious faiths that are represented in the department.

2. Sufficient experience in pastoral and parish work to cope with the spiritual, psychological and social needs of the members of the Department and the community.
3. Willingness to conform to departmental policy as set forth in rules and regulations, general orders or any other order where applicable (particularly those relating to the Chaplaincy Program).
4. Willingness to undergo special departmental training and instruction in areas which relate to the role and functions of a police chaplain.
5. Willingness to accept appointment as, and meet basic requirements for, a reserve officer, pursuant to departmental policy. In this regard, the Chief of Police may waive certain requirements governing all such appointments and may modify or limit the scope of responsibilities or services performed.

Now they knew I was, to a degree, one of them, working within fairly rigid requirements and within fairly structured areas of responsibility. When I left them I hoped they were saying to themselves, "Wow! This chaplain knows where it's at. He's involved and competent."

I didn't know if they were saying that. I was already on my way to my car to resume cruising. And I had my greatest weapon with me—love.

In Hawaii we have some warring families who shall go nameless so I can survive. The riot call came in over my radio. When I showed up at the scene, there were already about a dozen police cars there. The area was in Waikiki. (But it's all changed now, replaced by high rises.) It was a real case of blood, sweat and tears when I walked over. The police were standing between the two factions, while accusations were flying about them. The two groups really wanted to get to each other—the authority figures interfering with their beating up on the enemy only served to stir them greater.

"Here comes the police chaplain," bellowed a police

officer in the hopes of it having some calming effect. Not with this bunch. I knew them.

I walked right into the midst of one group and said, disgustedly,

"How embarrassing. All you making ass." This is a local expression similar to the standard "making an ass out of yourself."

They quieted down when they heard me speak their language.

"You–men," I continued, "you make me embarrassed I get call to come here."

I kept using the word "embarrassed." The more embarrassed I became as a spiritual figure, the more embarrassed they grew. Shouting turned to mumbling. Soon the silence itself became embarrassing. Officers standing around started to drift away.

I motioned to the family leaders to come over to where I was standing. After a moment of that "who, me?" game, they walked over and I talked to them about "how lucky we live in Hawaii."

They agreed. "Right on, man." "It was my fault. I was bummed out, lost my job." "No, I was really too beered up." The police cars drove away. Finished.

Puzzle: Find God's law hidden in this picture.

Back on the road–it was late night now–I parked near the main drag of Waikiki and walked. Two women strolled along. You get to know a prostitute when you see one, after awhile.

Not so long ago Waikiki had only high-priced call girls. They charged up to $500 a night. They frequented conventions and high-priced hotels, and had a steady clientele among wealthy people. It was done all very quietly; hardly anybody knew about them. Then in 1970 to 1972, the business hit a peak with the influx of prostitutes from the mainland. Streetwalkers were crawling all over the place. About half worked independently, half worked with crime syndicates.

They were quite a problem to tourists and residents alike. They were an annoyance. People hated them. I figured I would love them. Not physically—but in God's way, in the name of Jesus.

I walked up to these two girls.

"Hi. I'm with the police department."

I handed them each my card. They looked like they were going to panic. I turned to one.

"Hey, you're turning white, and that's a miracle!"

They're thinking, what kind of cop is this?

"I'm a minister for the police department—one of three ministers with the Honolulu Police force. If I can be of help, call me. Whatever you tell me is a privileged communication."

I never have to explain privileged communication to these women. They know what it is. They've all been busted. They have attorneys. They've been through the whole trip.

I smiled and went on my way. I purposely did not encourage further conversation. They would only have been suspicious of me. If I saw them on the street again, I'd just wave. They would remember me. They have learned to spot undercover officers, and they will remember I am the minister they met one night.

Another one I had seen before passed me, but then stopped.

"Good to see you again," I said, smiling. "Remember me?"

"Oh, yeah. You're the Jesus cop."

"Right. How are things going for you?"

"Busy as ever!"

I hid my shudder. "Good. If that's what you want. Any time you want to talk about something else, I'm ready. You know where to reach me. See you."

"Right."

She moved on, swinging her bag.

"Hey, Rev!"

She had turned around and was heading back toward

me. "You remember Rosie? She was with me when I met you before."

"Yes. What about her?"

"I want you to pray for her. She's hurtin'!"

"What's happening?"

"She's at Queens Medical. Her old man beat her up. He found out she's crawling with VD. She wasn't having her health checkup. So he really stomped on her. Her head's kicked in and she probably will have to be operated on to clean out the VD. Will you go to see her? I've got to turn a couple of tricks now with some dudes. See you later."

I understood what she meant about "old man." That was her pimp or procurer. The incongruity of it all, I thought. In one breath she'd ask me to pray, and in the next breath—well!

Before I got into the car, I resolved to see Rosie the next day. She cried like a baby as I held her hand and prayed for her. Nobody had ever done that before. Everything else, maybe, but not that. She kept glancing at the door hoping the pimp would not walk in. I figured I'd better make it short, gave her some literature, and told her to call me if she wanted to make a change. I heard later she broke away from the guy and split for the mainland.

I put that visit to Rosie on my weekly report to the personnel officer. That's a report that summarizes the types of activities the police chaplains get involved in—recruit orientations, counseling, luncheons, staff meetings, ride-along and patrols, funerals, etc., and the hours for each. Those reports must be read, I know, because the captain gave me a verbal pat on the back for apparently going that extra step in this case.

I do the same thing when I see police officers in action. Frequently I'm there but just as an observer, waiting to be called if they need me. I stand by and since I am uniformed, I am spotted and called if necessary. If the whole thing is settled, I often walk up to the officer and say, "Hey, well done. I'm not the one to tell you how to do things but I just want to say I like the way you handled that."

It means a lot to them to have a fellow officer, even though I am a chaplain, make a positive comment. We need to encourage and lift one another. Of course, if I'm asked, I will make a suggestion on how a situation could have been handled, and usually it is appreciated. Some even jot notes down for later use.

Back to my patrol. I was back in my parked car now and the radio was spluttering out its ceaseless messages. I sat for a moment to see what was going on when I heard a nearby rookie patrolman call in to Central.

"Need some assistance with a rather goofy situation here. Is the sergeant around?" He named the hotel. It was just a step away from where I was.

Rookies always ask for the sergeant, as if he was their mother, which he is for awhile.

I walked over to the hotel and entered the lobby. First thing I saw was this dude lying on a divan in the lobby. He was handcuffed to the furniture. The rookie was chatting with the hotel manager, who was explaining how he saw the man lying there. The manager had gone over to say something about moving on when he saw the handcuffs. He figured the man was under arrest and the arresting officer was holding him there while he caught up with somebody else. But after an hour he decided he'd better call the police, who turned out to be the patrolman and who in turn had called the sergeant.

The handcuffed man was out cold. We could not tell whether it was drugs or alcohol. Later we found out it was a combination of both, and really bad.

The sergeant walked in. "Smart aleck drunk," he said, unlocking the cuffs. "Let's get him dried out at Queens."

Rather than delay the sergeant, I offered to take the rookie and his charge in my car. At Queens we waited for a medic's report on the man's condition. "A few hours ought to fix him up." We left. I took the rookie back to where I got him. "See you, thanks."

Chaplain or chauffeur? Mediator or intruder? Policeman or Jesus' man? Man's law or God's law? What manner of being am I? What is a police chaplain? What does he do? How do handcuffs go with a clerical collar. When you throw the book at a lawbreaker, is it the Bible? Can an officer of the peace be an officer of Christian peace, or Jewish peace, or Moslem peace?

Before I try to answer these questions, all of which point to an apparent contradiction, let me get the car back to headquarters.

It was now 2:00 in the morning. I drove back hoping the radio would not come up with a juicy one before I got there. I made it. I returned the keys. No reports to fill out, except for the weekly one tomorrow. I took my supplies back to the locker room.

My appointment book was in my pants pocket. I checked it: A benediction at a police lunch day after tomorrow. A recruit's wedding same day. Three counseling sessions the day after that. Good! Nothing on. I could sleep late that morning.

Before I left I talked to a runaway from the mainland. Then I asked an officer, "Anyone in the tank?"

"Yes," replied the officer. "One or two I think."

I walked over. A young man was in there. The guard opened the door for me, and I went in.

When the guy saw me come in, he staggered over, arms outstretched and proceeded to vomit all over me. Beer was cascading down my uniform and my shoes. He slumped down on his knees, his hands clasped around my legs, face buried between my ankles, sobbing and heaving.

Here it was 2:30 in the morning. This guy was puking his guts out and crying his heart out at the same time. Why did I become a police chaplain? Let's add that one to the list of questions we have waiting.

Even though I was standing in the middle of filth and in the grossest of conditions, I felt I was a part of something very blessed.

The uniqueness of the Christian faith is its ability to penetrate the darkest hour with its own special light.

Now about those questions. I'm not a weirdo. There are many chaplains working with the police forces in America.

There is very little written on the subject. Few people know about the program. Some who do, think it is some public relations gimmick. Not so. This book attempts to take you behind the scenes and let you see for yourself what makes us tick.

CHAPTER TWO
The Police Chaplain Amidst Violence

One cannot help but wonder what would happen if all the police in the world were Jesus cops. Would violence disappear?

I doubt it.

The police chaplain can frequently be a modifying influence, either damping the flames of violence or preventing sparks from igniting further.

But the roots of violence lie deep within the society, and like doctors, the police are usually treating only the symptoms, not the causes. Until the underlying causes of violence are removed, the police chaplain will always feel out of the real action and more like the water boy at a football game, just being around in case needed.

Sometimes the being around makes the Jesus cop feel superfluous. Sometimes he plays an important role in the enforcement of justice.

One early Saturday morning I was sound asleep in a Waikiki hotel when I woke up to screaming. At first I thought I might have been dreaming and started to go back to sleep when I heard this unmistakable screaming, interspersed with a woman's voice moaning, "Oh, God, no!"

I looked at the clock; it was 5 o'clock. Still groggy, I got out of bed and, thinking it was probably a hold-up two floors down in the lobby, I reached for a .38 pistol I keep by my bedside.

I tore out of my room, gun in hand, and dashed down two flights of stairs that led directly into the lobby. I kicked the lobby door open just in time—John Wayne style. In the center of the lobby was the Japanese night clerk struggling with a black man who seemed to be twice his size. Off to the side was a young blonde woman on her knees, blood running down her face from a wound on the side of her head. The big man, at least six foot four, with flashy felt hat, cape with far-out threads, big stomper shoes, looking like "Super-Fly" and holding what they call a fat bat in his hand, was trying to hit the little Japanese fellow, about five foot three, who had climbed halfway up his back, straddling his waist and doing his best to hang on.

It did not take a Sherlock Holmes to realize what was happening. A pimp was beating up his prostitute and the clerk had come to her rescue. Just as I appeared on the scene, the big man managed to shake the little man off. I put my two hands on my gun, which is the way they train you now in the accurate firing of a weapon.

"I'm a police officer! Freeze!"

The big man wheeled around and I could actually see him turn pale.

"Hey, man," he pleaded, "I don't want any hassles." He put both arms straight up in the air. Here was a real, tough hood-type doing a 180-degree turnabout. He looked like he was going to faint.

"Turn around." My voice spoke cop rather than chaplain. I stuck the gun in his back.

Now about the gun. I always keep the safety lock in "on" position. Safety factor number one. Also, I keep the first chamber empty. Safety factor number two. And, I keep my trigger finger on the trigger guard rather than on the trigger itself. Safety factor number three. I encourage others to do likewise.

These are safeguards not only against accidental firing of the weapon, but against hasty judgment or overreacting. It's not that I don't have faith in God's protection, but I also have faith in the truth that God helps those who help themselves. And why ignore a gut feeling to having a gun, then hear God say one day as you lie there, "Well, Bob, I warned you."

I gave him a quick police frisk and I told the desk clerk to call a certain number to get additional police help.

We were only a few feet from the street and people had begun to gather. I had a strange cool feeling and realized there I was, standing naked except for my jockey shorts.

Little wonder, when two patrolmen arrived a second later they stood at the door wondering who were the bad guys and who were the good guys.

The younger of the two, a rookie, moved toward me and I had the agonized feeling that he had made the wrong decision. Then the sergeant came through with, "He's one of us," and I thought I heard him mutter something like, "believe it or not."

"Which one?" the rookie seemed unconvinced, looking at me standing there in my shorts. He shook his head, placed his own gun next to mine and said, "You better get dressed." He then put the cuffs on the pimp.

Despite the tenseness of the situation, people were smiling and nudging one another. I had the feeling I was back in Hollywood doing a corny comedy sequence. I waved acknowledgment to the sergeant and beat a hasty retreat, going up those same stairs even faster than I had loped down.

I wish I could say that I had helped calm the prostitute, bathed her wounds, and made her understand the sinfulness of her ways. I wish I could say I rode with the pimp back to the station and encouraged him to express his remorse and a desire to make a change in his life.

I just did what I had to do—I put on my pants.

When I went back down, the main characters had left and the desk clerk was giving a full report to another patrolman. An argument had started in the lobby between the girl and her pimp. She was tired, was coming down with a cold, and wanted to call it a night. But the pimp had lined up a military dude who was willing to go double money, he wanted a girl so bad. After a few "You will" and "I won't" exchanges, the pimp had pulled out his fat bat and started chasing her around the lobby, bashing her head in. That was when the little Japanese desk clerk got into the act—and where I later came in.

Nobody knew I was a chaplain. I had no opportunity to perform as a chaplain. Yet, here I was in the midst of violence.

I cite the incident in order to point out that the police chaplain is more often than not a policeman first, chaplain second, if indeed there is an opportunity to express the latter role. This opportunity needs to be diplomatically developed as the situation permits. There is no script saying, "Enter police chaplain." You have to keep your spiritual antenna up and create your own moment. But it's hard to be creative without your pants on.

I was just starting out to cruise with a patrolman one night when a call came over that a rapist had driven away from the scene of his crime in a blue Toyota, license plate such-and-such. When there's a change of shift, there are twice as many police cars on the road—those setting out and those coming in. So it was not surprising to get another call on the radio, within seconds, that the car had been spotted in the Kapahulu area, headed toward Fort Ruger.

That was the area we were in. We flipped on our lights, turned on the siren, hit the pedal, and tried to head him off. We spotted him and joined the chase. We must have hit 80 miles in those narrow streets. I've been in high-speed chases before, both as a hot-rodder and as a police chaplain. But this was ridiculous. I think I actually closed my eyes once or twice, squeezing through oncoming and parked cars and screaming around corners.

The sirens going and the lights flashing certainly added to the emotional pitch. Sometimes, when the element of surprise is required, it's a no lights, no siren situation. But, when the police want to throw a psychological scare into a fugitive, like now, lights and sirens help.

The man flipped off his lights and swerved into an empty parking lot. Instantly police cars converged on him. And the parking lot was full. I was one of the first out of the car.

I thought, "Here is a rapist." Now to me this is one of the most violent and despicable crimes. It is visiting a gross violence against another human being, especially a female who is somewhat helpless compared to a male, and causing not only possible pregnancy and disease, but psychological injury that can often be disastrous.

As a Chaplain, my first priority is for the person's eternal well-being. There are different ramifications of that. In your course of duty, you sometimes have to set that aside temporarily until you get to that position. At other times it's the first thing that ensues.

With each situation a Chaplain has to discern the immediate need, and be sensitive to the specific situation. There's no such thing as a police chaplain always doing this or always doing that. It becomes a matter of Christian ethics, as the Bible teaches us.

Now I prayed for the man. I prayed for the girl. I asked the Lord to make me sensitive to the situation. I asked that, while all the officers might be down on the guy, I might show some compassion.

The man just sat in the car as we approached. One of the officers opened the door and two others dragged him out. He was a military man, obviously under the influence of a few too many drinks. They handcuffed him and sat him on the ground. He said he was from Schofield Barracks.

Now I did not have on my police uniform. It was not mandatory that I wear one. I was dressed in aloha shirt and slacks. Nor did I have any police chaplain identification card, which had not been issued at that time.

I walked up to him and sat down beside him. The officers knew who I was so they did not say anything.

"I'm the chaplain for the police department. I thought maybe I could be of help to you."

He looked at me and he must have felt my sincerity, and not as if my statement was kind of a recording issued as standard operating procedure.

"Oh, thank God you're here!" He turned his position to face me better. "Man, I'm really in trouble."

"Did you rape the girl? You can tell me in confidence. I will not bring it up again. I'm not a police officer. What you tell me is confidential."

"Yes, I did." He shook his head slowly from side to side. "I don't know what came over me. The juice is scared out of me now—but I was drunk, and all I could think of was having this chick. Man, am I in trouble!"

"You sure are. You're in big trouble."

"I can get busted."

"You can get more than that." I paused to let it sink in. "Listen," I said, "I happen to represent the Lord. I'm here to give you help—to assist in you realizing eternal peace. If you want to realize what you have done and believe that by faith, in the name of Christ, you can be forgiven for this—at this very moment you can be, even though you must pay the penalty."

He looked me straight in the eye.

"I used to be very religious. Not anymore. If I turn to God now, it's because I'm scared."

"I can't think of a better reason to turn to God. If it takes this moment to make it happen, do it."

I reminded him that punishment in God's hands is a lot easier to take than punishment from man's hands. "You have to pay the price—whatever the court metes out to you. This is the law, and it is the Christian's duty to obey the law of the land. But with God you pay with peace of mind."

"Will God accept anything I say to Him, even though I come to Him only when I'm desperate for help?"

"The Lord is used to that. Do it. Don't think about it. If you're happy about it and realize the truth of it, do it. Don't try to argue yourself out of it."

"All right, let's go." Police arms reached down and lifted him to his feet. He looked surprised. For a moment he had escaped the reality of the situation.

"Can I see you later?" he asked.

I nodded to him.

Later at the central station, he was fingerprinted and booked and his base notified. I went back into the cell block and had another talk with him. He would not pray with me at the time, but promised to talk to the base chaplain. A military escort then arrived to post his bail and take him back to Schofield Barracks. I knew that he was now opened to a new alternative.

A day or so later, I called the army chaplain and told him the story to the extent that I had been involved in it. He was in touch with the man and said, "It looks good."

A few months later I chanced to speak to the same chaplain and learned that the man had made a spiritual restitution and was facing his penalty with morale high. The girl who was the victim in the case went out to talk to him. She was so impressed with the changes that had come over him and his humility before her which she felt genuine, that she dropped charges.

Now this may not be a dramatic witness by any means. But the Chaplain needs to be aware of a more subtle function.

Here's a guy—drunk, lonely, rapes a chick, cops make a bust on him. He's sitting shirtless, handcuffed, all these lights, and police officers standing around staring at him. He's scared to death and has nobody to turn to. The only person who brings solace to him is a Christian.

It could have been anybody, but in this case it was me who stepped out of this nightmare, sat down with him and cared about his well-being and peace of mind. A Chaplain looked him in the eyes. That's one thing I always do with these people—stand very close to them, look them in the eyes, and speak gently and softly, knowing that a soft voice not only turns away anger but fear as well. A Chaplain related to him in a quiet, strong and loving way.

Chaplains everywhere might focus on this. I know they do in many cities. They create a magnet with their compassion. Whether it's rape, homicide, a runaway, whatever the situation may be, in the midst of squawking police radios, handcuffs and flashing lights, they step forward and reach out with warmth and understanding, side by side with strength and authority.

No matter the nature of the violence, and no matter what police department, there is a greater strength than violence—as the Bible says, peace that passeth all human understanding (read Philippians 4).

Sometimes peace lies very close to the surface in a crime situation and all you have to do is peer below the veneer of violence to identify it and restore it.

Take gambling. In Hawaii, the Filipino culture includes many types of gambling, including cockfights as well as standard crap-shooting and card games. One room on famous Hotel Street in downtown Honolulu gets "hit" periodically for gambling. We had a stake-out on this place for several months. We had taken pictures of people going in and coming out at different times and then identified possible suspects with known histories of gambling convictions. We had gone to court to get 30 or 40 "John Does" (warrants) so they could be served on anybody. Then we had to time a raid with the leadership of the vice squad.

I was invited to come along. They always have to bring

two neutral observers: usually one from the district attorney's or prosecutor's department and either a police chaplain or another observor.

This time there were four police cars. One was a utility truck that appeared to be working out front but there were really cops inside with surveillance equipment ready to give the signal to converge.

In these matters speed is of the essence. There is always a lookout to give the alarm to his gambling colleagues and the police have to break in past the obstacles invariably erected in their way, in time to nab the gamblers before they ditch the cards, hide the money or shape up in other ways.

We used a patrolman I'll call Big Primo, a Samoan fellow who weighed nearly 300 pounds and towered over most of us at six foot three. He had a massive chest and stomach and loved to bash down doors and run through walls. That was his bag. He was an expert at it. He was really a nice quiet guy, but place him in a situation where he was the juggernaut and he became like a locomotive quietly building up steam. Then POW!

The lookout had just peered up and down the street and locked the door. Then we got the signal. Four police squad cars roared up, the doors flew open and we piled out. Traffic was sealed off. Big Primo, who was in the utility truck, stood in front of the locked door, turned his head to the side and flexed his chest and stomach. There was a splintering crash and everything went flying.

Big Primo stepped in. The lookout was waiting inside with a club. He judiciously let Big Primo pass but then conked the next patrolman in. He was then quickly subdued as the rest of us poured in.

When I entered, Big Primo was standing at the top of a stairway where a metal door had been installed. We did not know about this door. We could hear feet scurrying around above us as the gamblers were getting rid of the evidence and preparing to scatter.

Big Primo stood in front of this metal door and, thinking it was wood, let go with his frame once again. When it refused to give, he became furious. He cocked his fist and smashed it right through the metal. I could see the blood fly but not Big Primo. As if nothing had happened he continued to smash a wider opening, reached in, released the bolt and we all followed him in.

We were surprised to see a very docile bunch of gamblers instead of the hostile, glowering, sullen bunch we usually confront. Apparently, seeing this fist come through the metal door had really shaken them up. They had never seen this kind of power before. They just sat or stood where they were, quite meekly, really frightened.

I joined the officers making a quick check of the place. Some of the Filipinos came back in the window after seeing we had covered the roof and fire escape. We looked everywhere for money, cards, chips, etc. One toilet with the seat down actually yielded a small Filipino man—the toilet had been altered to convert it into an emergency hiding place, which was pretty stupid as that's a sure place officers will look expecting to find evidence.

I opened a file drawer and was surprised when a second drawer opened with it, revealing another occupied hiding place. A little four-foot-eight man climbed out.

By this time the Filipinos were beginning to smile as they saw the humor in their "game." I wandered around among them, speaking a calming word here and there and mentioning that I was a police chaplain. Most were not interested, or did not want to talk. Some were hardened gamblers who had been through this situation a number of times. However, others were newcomers who did not want their families or their girlfriends to hear about this.

These younger fellows were in a crisis situation. As a Chaplain I was able to talk to them on a person-to-person basis, reminding them of the direction in which true help could be found. Two or three of them really appreciated my being there, enough to give me their names and addresses so I could send them some material to read.

In this type of a raid, the police chaplain is there primarily as an impartial observer to enhance the court situation, that is, be an effective voice in court for the department.

There is a second reason why the Chaplain is often invited on these raids. He supplies a calming effect. Police are usually outnumbered by gamblers and there is a temptation to use violence, bash a few heads in, to gain a point of physical dominance in the situation. A police chaplain's presence provides a cooling influence.

This cooling effect is felt by both sides and so there is no doubt that violence is frequently averted.

As far as turning individuals on to Jesus goes, you never know, I cannot remember being contacted by those to whom I sent literature in this case. But, at least it was received.

Speaking of violence, there was one time I had to use Mace. I carry Mace as a defensive weapon; it is built into my flashlight. So when I point the flashlight, I am also aiming the Mace. When I hit another button Mace really hits and incapacitates someone.

One night I was coming off the Hotel Street beat, walking down a side street when I heard a muffled sound, moaning, thuds, more moans. It was coming out of a dark alley. I grabbed my flashlight and headed in.

What I saw was a pathetic sight. This young kid about 18 or 19, about six-foot-four, who I later found was high on booze, had somehow lured a rookie cop into the alley and beat him absolutely senseless. He was a mass of nothing. His clothes were torn off; he was unconscious and bleeding from just about everywhere.

It seems to be the big turn-on for the local tough guys. When a rookie gets careless, they do a job on him. They try to get him in a side alley and just pound on him. The big studs really enjoy that, especially with a five-foot-seven rookie cop who is no contest.

The kid wheeled around with extreme rage and hate in his eyes. He didn't care who was behind the flashlight. He came toward me. In the darkness he looked even bigger than he was. I detected fear in his eyes, as is so often the case with people who live in violence.

He swore at me and started lunging at me. I gave him a shot of Mace. I hit him right in the face, going into his mouth and eyes. He went right to his knees. He was gagging and screaming. I ran up the street and yelled for patrolmen I knew were a block away, knowing my assailant wasn't going anywhere for a bit.

They came on the scene, saw the rookie in a mass of blood, and grabbed this big guy like they were going to put an end to his misery right then and there. I heard one of them mutter to the other, "Chaplain," and they held off. An ambulance arrived and took the unconscious rookie to the hospital.

The big guy was shoved in the back of a police car and two officers got in back with him. Now when you have a police car like this where the back of it is caged, you don't need to accompany the prisoner. He's in until you let him out. So I knew what these two were about to do with this prisoner.

Sure enough, when I went down a couple of hours later to see him at the police station, he wasn't there. I was told, "He met with an accident. He's at Queens Medical." I went over there and found him. He looked worse than the beat-up rookie. Those guys had *just beat him silly.*

Yet I can look at it from a police viewpoint and their action is surely understandable. They see one of their own lying there and it is the human instinct for revenge. They cross the demarcation line of law and order and become self-appointed vigilantes. I don't agree with it. It serves no good. Nor does it serve God. But meanwhile it's there. And until man gets to the causes of violence in society and roots them out, violence is going to beget violence.

To keep this type of escalation of violence to a minimum, officers should show restraint and compassion for such a kid's problems and humble the kid mentally rather than physically. Maybe then a repentant attitude would develop. That's the greatest force against violence.

Here lies perhaps one of the greatest frustrations of the police chaplain. I knew these two officers were going to beat this kid but I could do nothing about it. Nor could I "squeal" on them later. I'd be "dead" with every cop on the force. That's one of the ironies of being a police chaplain.

If there was a gross violation, such as an officer pulling out a gun to shoot the kid, I would have to step in and intervene as best I could.

One police chaplain, who saw unnecessary brutality by policemen, got upset, said some disparaging remarks to the department, and quit. I feel that proves nothing and solves nothing.

We Jesus cops have to hang in there. We are known as chaplains. That affects the consciousness of all who know us. It elevates the situation—maybe only one degree at a time—but God is patient.

CHAPTER THREE
The Police Chaplain in the Midst of Other Cops

"Police chaplains, in our way of thinking, should be chaplains to police officers and concentrate on their problems."

This opinion, expressed by a New England chaplain, is echoed by many police departments throughout the country.

I don't happen to agree, but I understand why others feel that way. The department should come first, they say, and here I do agree. But there has been enough left over of me to serve the community, too, in both police departments I have served—Honolulu and Palm Springs—plus other occasions when I have visited other cities and assisted their police chaplains for a few days.

In some large cities the advantage of community contact by the police chaplains is recognized but staffing does not allow this. They have solved the problem in some instances by asking local clergymen to volunteer their services one day a month to be "on duty" to accompany police officers on certain types of calls.

This is a reasonable enough compromise, but far from the ideal situation where the moderating influences of the police chaplain can defuse smoldering neighborhood tempers that might otherwise be triggered by a uniformed presence.

Lest I appear to be showing a priority for the ride-along

and other community work as opposed to being a chaplain to police officers, let me devote this chapter to emphasizing the importance of the police chaplain's "inside" duties. It so happens that much of this "inside" work arises from riding along and beat activities.

When I have been riding with a lieutenant or sergeant anywhere from a couple of hours to an eight-hour shift, it is quite natural at some point for the conversation to drift to some personal problem that is bothering the officer.

A police chaplain should *rarely* take advantage of his captive audience and initiate a spiritual conversation with the officer he is riding along with. Let the officer do it. I mean this!

For the first couple of hours, the personal talk will probably not come up. Some officers are on the defensive. They are afraid they are going to get a sermon laid on them by the chaplain. But, then, when this does not happen, man-to-man or friend-to-friend communication increases.

There has never been a time, however, when I rode along with any officers that they did not initiate a conversation. And I mean *never.* There's always a need. They must express it to somebody. The resistance to that expression is zero when they are with a chaplain in whom they have confidence.

In Palm Springs there was an officer who really hated the ride-along program. He had an extreme dislike for rookie cops. He put police chaplains in the same ball game. When I rode along with him for the first time, I decided I was not going to get trapped in a normal routine, especially his. I would be innovative.

I decided to do something to shake him up—to rattle him out of his usual prejudice so we could be off on an equal level.

As we jumped into the patrol car, he scowled, told me to do this and don't do that, as if I were a kid. Then he noticed I was writing it down.

"What's that all about?" he growled, gesturing at my note pad.

"Oh, well, I'm so new at this, Chief White wants me to write down whatever is said to me so we can have a record of attitudes and ground covered."

This was true. I had taken the precaution of seeing the chief before and asking him to issue me such an order, which he gladly did.

Ten seconds later here was a different man. He welcomed me into his car and actually gave me a smile. The rest of that tour was just one big togetherness.

Now he may have done a good acting job, but the fact is that we at least communicated the rest of the night. You do not come across this prejudice too often, but when you do, think of some way to change the game. Don't play the other's game. Play yours. Try to make it a together-game.

Usually things go smoothly right from the start. The easiest ride-alongs are with rookie cops when they know the police chaplain has been with the department a number of years. They wind up asking a lot of questions.

"Exactly what does the police chaplain program entail?"

This is the way a police officer usually sets the scene to hit you with his problems. You tell him. Then he tells you.

He means this as an honest question and may not have any conscious motive to lay a problem on you. Maybe he has seen an announcement on the bulletin board about the existence of a police chaplaincy, and that's all. All of a sudden there is a police chaplain sitting beside him in the car. So he asks.

Then while you explain, something strikes home to him. The shoe fits. So he puts it on.

"I got this cousin. Man, he's got this family thing." And he tells me the story.

I know it is not his cousin's problem. It is his own. But I let him hide behind that ploy. Frequently, I know he knows I know. But we keep up the third party bit to keep it flowing.

Inevitably it comes to a point, though, where we reach an honest level of meaningful exchange. Then I bring it into better focus with, "You're rapping about yourself, right? It'll help us both if you take the mask off."

Ninety percent of the time he does. And we go from there.

Some obvious rules to follow when you get in a police officer's car:

- Be yourself
- Show warmth
- Be consistent
- Don't compromise your faith
- Act professionally

The police chaplain who adheres to these rules of behavior wins the respect of the officers he rides with. Those officers can have real fears about your being "some sort of ding-a-ling who is going to louse up the action."

If you are asked a question about some call you are going out on, and you are not sure or don't know, it is best to be frank and admit your ignorance. Most officers see right through a front you throw up, but will respect frankness. Some chaplains feel that just because of their calling they have to come on as if they have all the answers. ("I'm really together. I'm a holy man. I've got it all.") That's about the best way I know to trip yourself up.

When you honestly say you don't know, then when you talk about what you do know, you get a lot better mileage.

I remember one instance when the police officer and I developed such a good rapport the first time out that he confessed a crime to me. This was a rare event. Usually the officer will seek counseling by rapping about his wife, his children, his neighbors, or money problems.

In this case it all arose because of a money problem. He

knew where there was gambling going on and he was getting a rake-off. He needed money to make both ends meet, so he gave in to the temptation. Shades of "Serpico" and the New York City Knapp Commission! I suppose every city has this to some degree, but that certainly does not make it right. Thankfully, in Honolulu it's rare—Palm Springs, too.

This officer who confessed to being on the take did so after we had ridden around for a few hours, had dinner and made a few radio calls. He began by exercising his option of privileged communication.

"Chaplain Bob, can I tell you something in professional confidence?"

"You have my pledge to privileged communication," I assured him.

"I've been getting money from this dice game. I'm sorry I got started with them. I want out."

He told me the details. He wanted to talk to somebody. He needed to get it off his chest. And he wanted out. The solution was obvious—he needed to be transferred to another area. He would never have to tell anybody why. When I suggested it, he shook his head.

"Look, we're being very frank with one another." I looked him straight in the eye. "What is your personal relationship with Jesus Christ? You know I'm a Christian cop. You know where I'm at. I'd like to know where you're at. Fair enough?"

He hesitated. "Well, you know, I used to go to church but then after college I sort of dropped it. Me and my wife, we talk about it occasionally, but never have really done anything about it."

"OK, you are not into going to church but you realize that if you really had a total 'right on' relationship with our Lord that was personal—if you had communications going with Him—it would be much more difficult to be involved in areas that you find yourself in, which you know by your confession to be wrong. If you permit God to live within you, it is hard to do something that is not of Him if He has possession of your life."

He nodded and occasionally injected, "Right."

I was now ready to move in.

"I'd like to invite you to seriously consider having this kind of a personal relationship with Christ, by accepting the Son of God as the Lord of your life. Then, if these temptations come along on your beat, you are able to withstand them. Remember, the Bible says you are given no temptation that you are not able to withstand."

He gave me another nod.

"In our own strength we are weak, but God's strength in us is so powerful we can handle it. No hassles. No big trauma over it."

He agreed to apply for a transfer. He agreed to try church again. He got the transfer. And I occasionally still see him at church. He's a together person—with God—his family—and the department.

Domestic problems are the most common, but money runs a close second. Its leading to a crime, as in this case, is rare in my own experience, but I get it in many other ways.

One thing is sure. Police are underpaid. I would like to see their salaries practically doubled. The rookies are hurt most. By the time union dues, retirement, and this and that are taken out, the cash left in his hand is minimal, especially with today's high cost of living—and Honolulu's cost of living is ridiculous.

A lot of officers who talk to me about their financial troubles have told how they have to take a part-time job or their wife has to work. Some have to take weekend jobs, which take away about the only time they can spend with their families. In some cases, even their kids have to go to work on after-school jobs.

I wonder if there is a police system that does not suffer from police whose hands are out to criminals. No large departments will ever admit it, but they know the situation exists.

They are working on it in their own way, but there are even political pressures that work against these internal corrective efforts.

It all points to the weakness of man's system compared to the biblical system for conducting our lives.

One of the big problems arises when policemen go into debt. Then comes a loan shark or a high interest commercial house. And that only makes matters worse.

I don't know what the solution is. I know it is not easy these days for city halls to give pay raises, but this is one area where big dividends would be returned to the public in quality police departments, free of the eroding, corrupting pressures of economic woes.

Well, here I am dwelling on money problems when actually more problems start with weddings. Since I perform them for the police in my function as police chaplain, you might say I am to blame. I have no magic when it comes to tying the marital knot. Domestic problems can and do arise.

I like to encourage marriage ceremonies that are unique and special. I will suggest to couples who ask me to perform their marriage service as police chaplain that they choose a natural place, out in God's own church. In Hawaii where the weather is almost always nice, these weddings have been held at Lookout Point on Mount Tantalus, Diamond Head Crater, Kahala Beach, Haiku Gardens and other scenic spots. The backyard of a home has often been a lovely place to hold a wedding. Of course, if they belong to a church I refer them right back to their pastor, but it seems many young police rookies and their brides are not churchgoers, so I do the honors. If I am to be conducting the ceremony because they have no home church, then I go all the way from premarital counseling to a gift Bible.

They may not be a Christian couple but I still marry them, contrary to the refusal of some ministers. I remind such colleagues of mine that the institution of marriage was not created just for Christians. It was created for all of mankind. God instituted this for all people. Adam and Eve were married in the sight of God, but they were not Christians. If non-Christians ask me to refrain from mentioning this-or-that and to do so would compromise my own faith, only then do I refuse.

The premarital counseling is of value to young couples. Some have no one to talk to about the subjects that are covered: finances, sex, in-laws, careers, the wife's understanding of her husband's job, and many secondary ramifications of these subjects that can arise.

Weddings of police officers tend to be more serious than other weddings. They are more quiet, more solemn. They are still full of joy but there is a subconscious thought lurking beneath the surface that here is a young couple getting married and in a short time he could be a statistic and she a widow. Let's face it. A man in uniform is marked. He could wind up assassinated in some alley. So could John Q. Public, but the risks in that uniform are very much greater.

I try to reassure the couple prior to marriage by pointing out the benefits of a relationship to the Lord and the eternal life we can have with Him . . . I'm getting ahead of myself. Let me back up to the initial counseling.

With money the important factor that it is in a policeman's life, I usually like to see a couple squared away in this department. I remember one couple—both Honolulu kids. He was a junior college graduate, she had a year of college. She looked forward to being a homemaker. She was planning to quit her job just before the wedding and take up this new career. They both agreed upon it.

I made them add up their rent, food, car and other essential expenses. The sum came to $80 more than he would be earning.

"You know what that means?" I asked. "Finance companies, loan sharks, and bankruptcy."

"I never realized this," he said.

"Me, neither," she agreed.

"I strongly recommend," I urged, "you either wait for that raise you will soon get automatically, or . . ." turning to her, "that you find a job instead of making this fellow hold down a job and a half."

They expressed their agreement and promised they would think it over, but I sensed they did not like what was coming out of this process called counseling. They were bothered.

I was relieved when he called for another appointment. They had a different attitude. It was one of thanks. They had talked it over with her parents, who had never really thought about this factor, assuming working for the city would be economically supporting. It was decided she would work part time. She got a job at a local department store and they waited a few months until his raise was imminent. Meanwhile, she liked her job, they liked her, she decided to continue working and she, too, got a raise.

So, when I conducted the ceremony, a cloud over the event was "all pau" (no more).

Perhaps you are thinking that I acted as an accountant in this case, not as a minister. But I am bringing out the essence of the counseling. Actually, it is always packaged in spiritual terms, not as a sermon. But reference is continually made to God's eternal principle.

It is not wise for man to have a home that he may lose. A servant is worthy of his hire. If you do not work, you do not eat. A man's family is his responsibility and he is held accountable to God. You don't hear an accountant talking exactly this way.

When a statement is made in counseling which contains sociological advice, unless it has biblical foundation, in my opinion the counseling is worthless as spiritual counseling. What does it profit a man to have marriage and a home, if he ignores spiritual truths—and economic truths are part of spiritual truths—and loses it all. God instituted the principle of "providing." Our faith is in Him and He provides. Some people may say, "Well, I have no faith, and I get by." But that does not change the principle. God wants us to survive. We have the choice of working with Him or against Him.

Then there is sexual counseling for the recruit or officer and his bride-to-be. There are times when couples will talk quite freely about this subject. Frequently there has been mutual sexual involvement already. I feel I must touch all the bases in justice to those who come to me to sanctify a marriage—police personnel or not.

On occasion I may ask the bride if I can speak to her husband alone. Then I may say to him, "I get some vibes that you got something going on the side or else you may intend to."

When I get that feeling I am usually correct. But even if I don't exactly strike oil, it opens up the conversation so we can place the whole physical aspect of love into a spiritual frame of reference.

Quite often I get a sunset red glow from the fellow. That's reply enough.

"How can you go into an equality, a sensitivity, a togetherness when you are out making it with other women?"

The red glow usually yields to the somber gray of shame. He knows within himself that by playing around he is heaping dirt upon his wife. Sometimes it is the other way around. But my approach is exactly the same.

About the sexual act itself, I dive right into the subject unabashed. That attitude helps. If a pastor looks very uncomfortable or if he fusses and stews around, fumbling for the right words, the young people are going to react nervously and be uptight. I come out matter-of-factly and just as point-blank on this subject as others.

"OK. That takes care of Chapter One. And we have taken care of Chapter Two, finances. Now how about Chapter Three? This is where it's lots of fun. We're going to talk about sex."

Usually we all laugh. A nervous reaction, but a positive one, letting go of the uptightness.

"That's a very important part of marriage. Did you know that?"

More laughter, and giggles.

Maybe he'll say, "Right on."

And I'll look at her and say approvingly, "I agree with you, right on. This is a cutie. And your groom looks like he may be a tiger, too."

More laughter and everybody is relaxed. Then I am able to get down to business.

"Do you realize that it says in the Scriptures that when a man marries, his body no longer belongs to him? It belongs to his wife. We are taught this in the New Testament. Very few Christians know this."

"No, I didn't know that," he may reply.

Then I turn to her. "And you, young lady, the same applies to you, according to the Scriptures. A wife's body belongs to her husband. The idea is that the body is a symbol of the self. You give your heart when you say, 'I do.' The body is for the pleasure of the other person. Concentrate on pleasing the other person and not merely yourself and that mutually reflects in other aspects of your marriage."

The purpose of counseling in this area is to bring it into the spiritual framework where it belongs. If I leave it out, so might they. That is, they might not see how God's laws have jurisdiction in this aspect of their life. So they might mentally leave it—sexual behavior—out in the social scene where they found it in the first place.

A cop has things tough enough with prostitutes offering their services free, frail young chicks playing up to him, and the attractiveness of the man in the uniform. But don't think that is not part of his own self-image. And don't think she is not aware of it.

We have a delicate balance here, and who is better able to handle it than a person who understands the cop—while at the same time talking God's language?

Sometimes the police chaplain uncovers an incompatibility lurking beneath the surface. A disinclination to talk about something, a flush, a knowing glance—and you know something is not right. Often you are able to root it out, and then they can decide "where do we go from here." I have had two cases where, after counseling, the marriage was off. In both cases, they decided between themselves they would not make it. One was a case where they were sexually compatible to the *nth* degree, but they had nothing else going for them. In the other case, they disagreed on everything but were trying to be polite to each other. They saw through it in the counseling and how the festering would soon break the covering.

One unusual counseling situation arose when I had a call from a police officer who asked if I could counsel a young nephew and his fiancee. Although this was somewhat beyond the call of duty, I agreed. When I arrived at the officer's home, I found I was expected to "do my thing" at the dinner table with the officer-uncle and his wife, the aunt, present, making—with the groom and bride-to-be—five at the table.

The conversation started off gingerly, but I saw right away that the young lady was a Christian and spiritual in her thinking, while the young man was, weakly, the follower. The Bible says the man is the head of the home. If the man cannot be at least the spiritual equal of his wife, to me that spells incompatibility. The man is responsible for the spiritual welfare of his family. Here was a young man who was agreeable to turning that responsibility over to his wife. I came out bluntly when that point became evident.

"Do you know that you are going to cause irritation and frustration in your relationship by not being 'with it' spiritually?" I asked him. "She may not know why, but it will be because you are not showing the spiritual strength expected of the male—indeed ordained by God."

He said he was unaware of this responsibility. We checked the Bible and I showed him the passages. He was a believer but not religiously inclined. He seemed impressed. She lit up.

"You know, I respect my 'husband', but somehow there is something missing in that respect."

"Yes," I reminded her, "the Bible does not say that wives should first love their husbands, but they must respect them. If a woman doesn't respect her husband, she won't love him—for that's her nature. The man needs to love before he respects. By the man loving and the woman respecting, together, they unify."

They did not realize what had loomed between them until it was pointed out. Then they reacted so positively that the police officer and his wife, who did not think that this was of any importance, began to look seriously at it, too. They all came together that evening on the subject of our Lord. It was as if there was a sixth setting at the table that night.

Net result: the young man's attitude changed toward church. He attended and read the Bible. He became enthusiastic about acquiring spiritual knowledge and strength. After the wedding, she said to me, "I feel completed as a woman."

Premarital counseling is only part of the story. Married couples can have rough going when the husband is on the police force.

With the rookie wife, fear is the biggest problem: fear for the safety of her husband. The old-timer gets used to it. The long hours don't help. She gets torn between thoughts for his safety and those torturing doubts: is he making it with another woman?

Most of these young wives have learned to unload their tensions on other young wives, rather than upset their husbands. They form little pockets of self-help. But it's like the blind leading the blind. The listener is just as worried about her husband, so there is no satisfaction there. She cannot go to another police officer, doing so might jeopardize the husband's job. When they eventually call me the first thing they say is, "Don't tell the Captain."

If I hand this woman that old sweet talk, "Don't worry about it, now. Think good thoughts. Support him all the way," then walk out the door, I'd be handing her a lot of nothing.

What the police chaplain has to give in such a circumstance is the ultimate answer: our Lord. The peace that God can give. I leave a Bible with her, or we read from the Scriptures together right then, or we pray together. Sometimes I recommend other women whose spirituality, wisdom and maturity could be of some assistance to her.

We also handle the problem straight-on. She should go to him and say, "Honey, you are my husband. I owe it to you to tell you all the things I feel. I assume you want to know. I'm probably just a silly little wife but these thoughts keep coming to mind . . . " and then tell him. If she cannot do this, then there is a deeper underlying problem between the two that interferes with communications. Address your counseling to identifying and handling that basic problem and the other will most likely disappear.

Later, the police officer or rookie will often contact me. His wife has spoken to him. He was surprised she thought that. He understands how the wife is at home and she has these fears. He is thankful she talked to him so honestly about it. I never hear from the cop who does not have it all together and who reacts to his wife's fears with, "Oh, that's stupid," and walks out on the conversation. But, it has happened. Then the communications problem is back, but it's his, not hers.

Here's a typical counseling session between police chaplain and police officer. We've been riding around a few hours, stopped for a number of radio calls—and a snack—and the watch is nearing its end. We'll both be glad to get home and relax. Then he suddenly turns to me.

"Bob, I get home and I'm wiped out. My old lady wants to go somewhere. All I want to do is hit that sack. I've been zippin' around this town, hitting all these spots, working overtime. I stagger home after twelve hours. She's home bored, watching television, just waiting for me so we can go out to dinner or visit people and do something. It's a constant clash between us."

"It's a common problem. I get it often," I reply. And to prove I understand, I give it back to him. "The cop has been talking all day long, gets home to a chance for some quiet and there she is waiting to tell him about three thousand things."

I have his ear now. That's exactly the problem. The chaplain understands.

"So, what's the answer? What does a guy do?"

"Compromise," I reply.

"Compromise your true feelings?"

"Not exactly. Compromising in the sense that you are sensitive to your wife's needs and she to yours. Maybe you come home, have a nap for an hour, shake it off, and get cracking. She needs to realize your need for this, or your need for a period of quiet for awhile. She backs up. Then you both go ahead—together. Or, you have a chat first, giving her a chance to let off steam. Then you take your nap. It's a mutual compromise. You each make a little sacrifice of your personal emotions for the other's benefit."

Most couples flash on this as the right way. They just never pick up on it until they hear a third person talk about it. Then it makes sense.

Most of these cases that the police chaplain is made privy to have gotten to the argument stage. Whatever the reason behind the argument, I point out what's happening.

"When you argue with your wife, aren't you so busy trying to get your point across you are not really listening to what she has to say? That's what arguing is. But the next time you are arguing, say, 'You give me your point while I listen carefully, then I'll give you my point while you listen carefully.' The whole argument scene changes suddenly.

When you try to understand the other person as much as you try to get them to understand you, a resolution becomes possible. Barriers drop. Who is right gives way to what is right.

"Sound like Jung or Freud? Guess again. It's a Bible principle. It does not have to be wrapped in thees and thous to work."

"That's in the Bible?"

"Sure. Do you have a Bible? Want a copy? I'll drop one off to you later this week. Here are some spots to check." I scribble off a few references.

Whatever the principle I bring out in counseling, that's where it comes from.

"Hey, where did you get that principle from? It's right on."

"From Moses."

"Is he new on the force? I haven't met him yet."

The police chaplain rubs shoulders with other cops at banquets, funerals, or weddings. He sees them from the time they are police cadets to the time they hang up the uniforms for the last time.

But the time he "sees" them the closest—the time when he is really in their midst—is when one turns to him and says,

"Chaplain Bob, can I talk to you about something?"

CHAPTER FOUR
Duties Of The Police Chaplain

Suicides have become the third highest cause of death among young people between the ages 15 to 24, according to statistics. Formerly, more victims of suicide were in the middle-age bracket—the overburdened businessmen.

The Reverend Jack Price, chaplain of the Albuquerque Police Department, recently reported to the International Conference of Police Chaplains on a survey he did through 20 other chaplains in the United States and Canada. All were facing an increasing number of youthful suicides.

A chaplain from Rockford, Illinois, reported that an 11-year-old had killed herself. The Reverend Charles Massy, who works with the Royal Canadian Mounted Police, reported there were "more of these cases than I care to think about."

The timely presence of a chaplain might help prevent a suicide. Certainly he could soften the blow to the next of kin.

List suicides as an important duty of the police chaplain.

However, it is not a simple matter to get agreement from every police department that this is so. Some departments see the duties of a police chaplain as solely an internal matter—the moral and spiritual well-being of members of the department and their families. Period.

Other departments see the potential community good that the police chaplain can do by being in the right place at the right time.

How does a police department go about defining these duties?

That was the problem the Palm Springs Police Department had when I first interested Chief Robert White in establishing a police chaplaincy. Let me tell how it all developed.

In January, 1974, contemplating about a one-year move from Honolulu to Palm Springs, California, I decided to introduce myself to Chief White. He was available and I was shown into his office. A tall man with a ruddy complexion, Chief White looked as if he had seen his share of duty as a front-line officer. He was soft spoken and polite and I liked the way he looked me in the eyes and listened intently when I spoke.

"I expect to be a resident of Palm Springs in a few months," I said, showing him my badge and ID card from the Honolulu Police Department. "Do you have a police department chaplain here?"

"No," he replied with interest, "at one time we had a chaplain member of the Riverside County Sheriff's Department discuss a program with us, but it never got off the ground."

I described the program I was part of in Honolulu and said I would be glad to set one up in Palm Springs.

"It would not be the same," I explained. "There are differences that would have to be reflected in how we would proceed."

Chief White thought for a moment.

"There's a man I think should be in on our conversation. He is in charge of our community relations. His name is Ted Greene."

When Lt. Greene joined us, I reviewed the program—counseling, follow-up, ride-along—answering questions by both men.

Then Chief White asked, "Do you want to be salaried?"

"No," I replied. "I already am salaried. I am not looking for a paying job."

Chief White sat up straighter in the chair. He seemed more interested than ever. I sensed he had thought I was looking for a job and that he was not evaluating the potential good of the program as much as the potential cost. He later confirmed this. At any rate, the conversation now flowed more easily.

In describing how I raised my own support, I said, "It's similar to Campus Crusade for Christ, an organization not too far from here in San Bernardino."

"I know that organization," exclaimed Ted Greene, "I've been up to a number of their retreats."

A brother, I told myself. And when Chief White was interrupted by a phone call a moment later, Ted and I gave each other the "One Way" sign.

Chief White then gave me the go ahead. "Spell out exactly what you have in mind and when you are settled here, let's get to work on it."

Ted and I chatted some more in another office. He explained that out of some 80 officers, there were only one or two mature Christians. We prayed together in his office right then and there. We dedicated that situation to the Lord.

I stopped by again in June to say, "Hello," but in September I had completed my move and had prepared a list of duties and responsibilities of a proposed Palm Springs Police Chaplaincy and simple administrative procedures for implementing it.

"OK, let's get moving," said Chief White. "To make this legal, you'll have to become a reserve police officer."

I went through the program and this included being interviewed by their reserve officers' review board. They were very polite and very straightforward. They examined a lengthy form I had been asked to fill out. On it were a number of questions on bank accounts and finances which I had replied to with one word "personal."

One officer commented, "You like to keep a number of things personal, don't you?"

"That's right," I replied. "If you were paying my salary and I was becoming an employee, I would see the need of sharing such information. But I am a volunteer."

"No problem," was the reply.

Next came the key question which I have found to be the most sensitive area of the whole concept of the police chaplaincy.

"Well, the purpose of becoming a police chaplain is what—to become a police officer?"

"Not at all," I replied firmly. "Police chaplain, not police officer—assisting the police only on request."

"On request?"

"For instance," I explained, "suppose I'm riding along and there's a domestic quarrel. I'm right there and available. If the officer wants to handle it himself, fine. But I'm there as backup. If he feels a chaplain could help to calm the situation down, he tells the couple, 'I'd like our chaplain to talk to you.' "

I went on to reassure the board members that I would be involved only when needed and that would be ascertained by the officer in charge, not by me. I gave more examples from modus operandi in Honolulu.

"Would you take another human life, if you had to?" The question, put to me by a captain, I recognized as the last question on the questionnaire I had filled out. I had answered "yes." Now he was apparently asking me to elaborate.

"Yes, if I had to," I replied, "if it came to a showdown between me or the other guy—I don't see any glory to God with my being wasted. Not to bail out on this thing, but it would have to be a last resort's situation."

"Do you think you should carry armament?"

"No, I do not. It would invalidate my presence as a police chaplain. But I do think chaplains should carry Mace. In that way we can better carry out the buddy system and be of increased value should an officer be jumped. It's a defensive weapon, anyway."

These statements seemed to appeal to the board. They brought up the subject of uniform last. I expressed my opinion that the police chaplain should wear, as close as possible, the same uniform that a police officer wears. "In Honolulu, they don't allow this," I noted, "but I don't agree."

I was accepted by the review board. Chief White went on to touch all the bases. I consulted with the City Manager and other city departments.

One official, hearing I was a volunteer, asked, "I'm just curious. What do you get out of this?"

"Satisfaction in getting this program underway in Palm Springs. It will help the community. If it helps the community, it also helps me."

No more questions.

The way was finally cleared. I received the OK on a police uniform—exact hat, trousers, belt, shoes, shirt. The only thing different was the badge. Instead of saying patrolman or officer, it said "Police Chaplain." And, instead of a tie, I wore a clerical collar.

Still, my duties and responsibilities were not defined. "Let your experience in Honolulu be the guide," Chief White suggested. So we played it by ear.

I would get into uniform and report to the watch commander, identify myself and be assigned to a car. I would then ride with that officer. It was a duty that many police chaplains throughout the country have still not been given.

Of course, I gave the desk my phone number with the instructions that I be called for all emergencies. I also sent a mailer to all police officers informing them the program was underway and I was on call for personal or community matters. It was a follow-up to a memo the Chief had already sent out to department heads, but the memo was not very explicit about my duties. So this follow-up was necessary to explain my background and what my activities in Honolulu consisted of. I emphasized family situations within the department and backup "on request." It was low key: "Call us when you need us."

We got off to a great start. The Chief "suggested" that every officer have me along for the ride-along experience. That was a fine decision on his part as, left to the whim of the individual officer, the whole process could have stretched over a long period. As it was I got to know many of the officers in a short time. And they got to know me. The word soon got out that Chaplain Bob Turnbull was OK. I don't know what they expected—maybe prayers, hymns and blessings every block—but all they got was the kind of friendly conversation they would have from anybody else riding along. Stories about "action" I'd seen in Honolulu helped, I think. Chaplains may be spiritually qualified, but if they are not the gutsy type, they can be "shot down" by the men on the force. Anyhow, I didn't have that problem!

My first opportunity to show a police chaplain in action was in the arrest of a prostitute. The girl had just turned her first trick. Her customer had passed a bad check at a hotel desk and it was about him that the call had come in. This guy had a record and there was a warrant out for him in northern California. And when the officer kicked the door in, he had two arrests to make.

She was hysterical. The first job out, she gets "busted." The fact that I turned up with the officer at this moment gave her real pause. I don't think she actually accepted me as the "hand of God," but neither do I think she ever got back into her "profession."

Preventive medicine is a seldom used "tool" of the police chaplain but let me give an example at this point—because it, too, involved hookers, or in this case "call girls." The basic difference between the two is really price. A hooker is a street-type girl. Her price is low and her volume high. The call girl is higher priced—even 500 and up to 1000 dollars, but she'll stay the night or longer.

Wherever the golf classics go, there is big money, and Palm Springs is no exception. I was riding with a somewhat new cop one Wednesday when we got to talking about this, because the Bob Hope Classic was starting the next day.

"There are two now," I said pointing to two tall classy-looking blondes getting out of a cab in front of a hotel.

"How can you tell?" he asked.

"Watch," I said, "as I spoil their weekend."

We parked nearby. I buttoned up my coat so my clerical collar would be hidden from view and I took off my badge so I would not be identified as a chaplain. We followed them in. They had just registered as we walked up to them. One was a true platinum blonde. As she looked at me I saw her face drain of color. The other girl looked around at me and at this uniformed policeman with me and she obviously was angered by the sight. She was the cop-hater type.

"Good evening, ladies," I sang out cheerily, "welcome to our city. I take it you are visitors." My voice was so overly friendly it was caustic.

The cop-hater type turned away, but the platinum blonde replied, "Yes, we are."

"You know there is a lot of danger that lurks the streets. As in any city, there are all types of people. We want you to know that you are going to be protected here. My buddy and I, as well as other members of the police force, are going to watch you night and day."

I glanced at my rookie friend and could see he was having all he could do to keep a straight face.

"I want you to feel safe and secure," I continued seriously. "No harm will befall you in this fair city."

The other woman had walked away. She was so mad she was sputtering and swearing under her breath. "I'm sure we'll be OK," the platinum offered meekly.

"Tisk, tisk," I said, purposely pronouncing the words, not just clicking my tongue. "You can never be too careful.

Now, you may not see us but we'll we around. Should anybody bother you or knock on your door, we'll handle him. You are fine young ladies and we want you to have a good time. Don't bother to thank us. This is just the courtesy of our Department."

And we walked away.

"Man, you just ruined their business," chuckled the officer as we drove off. "They are probably still grumbling to themselves."

This may sound like a rude approach. And I'm not offering it as a standard operating procedure or even within the scope of a police chaplain's responsibilities or duties. It was just my way of taking preventive action. Why make prostitution easier? The harder it is, the more likely they will find a more productive life-style. Those two, I'm sure, still hear footsteps.

"Hey, that's neat," was the reaction of other police officers when the incident was later related. They agreed it took a probable situation crime, or lawlessness, and eradicated it before it could come about. Possibly, anyway.

Here the police chaplain, in this case me, came up with an "offbeat" approach that proved effective.

This is the principle that I want to bring out, not just the specifics of the above example. Insert the chaplain's approach into some standard law enforcement situation and you can come up with a novel solution which might prove to be easier on all concerned, including the taxpayers, than the standard solution.

I'm not saying the policemen cannot be innovators. I have seen some ingenious solutions to enforcement problems originate with beat cops. But the chaplain can add to this ingenuity, given the chance. It may not be his duty to do so. But it is his obligation.

Lest you think I am advocating "far-out" duties of an innovative nature for the police chaplain, let me hasten to provide a list of basic duties that are more on target.

I like the way this was done in Spokane. Their one-man police chaplaincy got started when a member of the clergy volunteered, pretty much as I did in Palm Springs. Except, in Spokane, the problem of where the chaplain ends and policeman begins was still fuzzy.

"Our first volunteer wanted to wear a police uniform and have firearms training," recalls Lt. Jack Tenney, community relations officer for the Spokane Police Department. They drew the line on police uniform but provided an ID card and name plate. Training was spelled out as either night training with Civil Defense police or selected classes at the police academy recruit school. There was also to be some in-service training. The department supplied office space and a portable radio transmitter receiver.

Duties of the new chaplain were outlined as follows:

1. Provide liaison with other religious leaders in community.
   Examples—keep in contact with different religious bodies;
   —attend monthly ministers' meetings and/or coordinate its activities.

2. Conduct memorial services and communion breakfasts.
   Examples—for retired officer passed away;
   —for officer killed in the line of duty.

3. Provide assistance to families in the event an officer is injured or killed while on duty.

4. Officiate at dinners and social events.
   Examples—any official police function (guild).

5. Visit the sick or injured personnel and/or families at home or in the hospital.
   Examples—list could be kept of sick or injured;

—take care of needs in home or hospital as they arise.

6. Counsel officers with personal problems.
   Examples—marriage problems;
   —other family or religious matters.

7. Represent officers before official bodies, on request.
   Example—disciplinary board, officer could request chaplain to speak on his behalf.

8. Attend funerals, officiate if requested.
   Example—family of officers killed on duty could request service.

9. Community relations activities, public relation efforts.
   Examples—respond to minority problems, neighborhood disturbances;
   —become known as police chaplain throughout community.

10. Ride patrol with officers as advisor and observer in community relations and minority problems.
    Example—assist as needed at accidents or on house calls.

11. Conduct in-service training classes, attend roll call.
    Examples—get to know officers;
    —teach how to deal with emotional problems.

12. Attend graduation and swearing-in ceremonies.

This is a well-balanced delineation. It covers internal and community areas of work.

If one is not familiar with the police from an insider's point of view, the above duties may seem to heavily focus on death or injury to a police officer, which is very traumatic for the whole department when it occurs. Just like every airline pilot's wife cringes at the news of a fatal crash ("There but for the grace of God . . ."), so the death or serious injury of a police officer in the line of duty strikes deeply into the hearts and minds of every man, woman and family in the department.

If solace is not provided, and faith restored, the wounds can fester.

Let me describe one such tragedy in Palm Springs. A 21-year-old police officer, who had graduated number one in his class in September, was killed in an off-duty collision the following March. Somebody just plowed right into him. He was killed instantly, his date badly injured.

I got a call from an officer at about 10 P.M. and I was asked to inform the parents about the tragedy. I immediately checked in at the station where I picked up the necessary information and details. A sergeant and a lieutenant went along with me.

We drove up to the house just before midnight. There were lights on. As we walked up, the mother had just come out the side door. She saw us approach.

"Yes?"

She answered her own question. Two officers and a chaplain don't just show up at your house at midnight, unless . . .

"Are you Mrs. Smith?" (Names have been changed for this account.)

"Yes, I am."

"Are you the mother of John Smith?"

"Yes, I am."

She answered matter-of-factly, but you could tell she already surmised, but was not ready to accept the news.

"Is your husband home?"

"Yes, he is."

"May we come in?"

"Yes, you may."

"God help her," I said to myself, "and me."

We followed her into the living room. There was a teenage boy in the room, the deceased's younger brother. The woman went up to her husband and clutched him.

"Honey," she said quietly.

What I said next was a standard statement. Some people may think it too cold and harsh. But I have been trained this way and I see its advantage. You say it directly and hope for shock to set in. While this natural sedative is operative, you can cover a lot of other necessary ground that might otherwise be too painful.

"Mr. and Mrs. Smith, I'm Chaplain Turnbull from the Palm Springs Police Department. I'm very sorry to have to inform you that your son John was killed in a car wreck about three hours ago."

The mother collapsed in her husband's arms.

The father kept repeating, "Why? How could this happen? Why? Why? We just saw him this evening. And his girlfriend. How is she?"

"Severe brain damage. She's in the Palm Springs Hospital right now—being transferred to Riverside Community Hospital."

I answered directly. I offered no personal opinions on how "terrible" the thing was I had to tell them. I left out emotions. I came on BOOM, yet compassionately, lovingly, kindly, softly, but directly. It was the fourth time I have had to do this, and each time it has proven to be the right way.

"We need to make certain arrangements at this time. Do you have a family doctor?" They did not. "Do you have a family minister?" No, they did not.

"Do you wish the department to make arrangements for the funeral?"

"Yes, please."

The other officers then joined the conversation explaining how the funeral would be in three days and they should check with the department. The important thing was to keep talking at this moment. Keep the discussion going, to keep their minds off the full realization for awhile, and let time work its healing.

When we left a few minutes later, all three members of the family were in a state of shock, but the numbness helped them to fall asleep that night and be in a better physical condition when the real mental shock waves hit them.

Meanwhile, I consulted with the mortuary and set funeral plans in motion. Assisting me with these arrangements was Jeff Sanders, who was director of the Palm Springs Chaplaincy with which I was affiliated. He had become a police chaplain with me. He's an Oral Roberts University graduate, who had joined our ministry.

If you can use the word in this context, it was a super funeral. The Sheriff's Academy, having been informed by the Palm Springs police that one of their recent graduates had been killed, sent police cars with representatives from all over southern California. They formed the honor guard—60 police cars with flashing red lights.

The cadets were there and observed. The parents were seated by the casket. A police officer's wife sang some Christian songs and played the autoharp. First, Jeff read a few Scripture verses. Then I gave a message based on Abraham Lincoln's statement that it is not the dead that we are here for but the living. I had discussed this previously with the parents and got their permission to point out that we were not there to pay honor to somebody who is no longer here.

"How many present wish they had said the kind words they had thought but never voiced and now find it's too late? Let us profit by this and pay honor to those we respect. Talk to people. Be open in your communications. Say a kind word. Pay your respects to the living."

It was an affirmative, evangelistic kind of message to those that remained.

"John is a Christian. So he is with our heavenly Father.

I really cannot feel sorry for him. Let's turn that compassion instead to our fellowman—to the living."

Later the parents and the brother wrote thanking the department for "help when we needed it so much . . . The funeral was handled in a very beautiful and dignified manner . . . It helped much to ease our sorrow for the loss of a much loved son and brother."

Unspoken, of course, was the boost to police morale, the indirect effects on performance and recruitment, the police image in the community, all areas of potential contributions by any police chaplaincy.

Earlier in this chapter I quoted Spokane's Police Chaplaincy duties because they are so well-balanced and succinct.

There are gray areas that are also important but not so easy to spell out. Here are four examples from the Honolulu Police Chaplaincy program.

- Development of relationships with officers and staff which may enable chaplains to foresee personal problems in the making and to deal with them before they advance to critical stages.
- Cultivation of good relations between the Police Department and the general community and opening channels of communications with other agencies.
- Visiting departmental elements to get acquainted with employees on a personal basis.
- Calling upon Field Operations watch commanders to secure assignments with on-duty sergeants or beat men so that they may meet more officers and become more familiar with problems confronting officers during their tour of duty.

A hard-nosed administrator might question the direct benefits attainable from these. Some of these points are in the nature of "preventive medicine," a luxury in these days of trying to keep up with the problems already manifest.

Perhaps we will not be able to ever catch up with these problems unless we do see the value in preventive work—nipping them in the bud so to speak.

The police chaplain can spot a furrowed brow and a preoccupied look as skillfully as an officer can spot a concealed weapon. He also has special skills in getting a person to talk about the smoldering anxiety. Scratch one more divorce. Or one more financial mistake. Or one more absentee.

As for good relations between the police and the community, no administrator will argue about the need for this, but no two administrators are likely to agree on step-by-step procedures to attain them. The police chaplain is not the only answer but he is a positive factor contributing to this goal. Pushed to the wall to explain how he will proceed, the police chaplain is probably as much in the dark as anyone else as to just how to delineate a specific community program. But left on his own, he will generate goodwill spontaneously in direct proportion to the amount of time he is able to give to police-community relations.

"Visiting departmental elements" and "meeting more officers" on duty may seem like interference with efficiency to some administrators, or maybe even going soft. But, call it what you may, any reminder of a person's spiritual nature and the security that implies, even if that reminder is merely a chaplain's collar, can be reinforcing.

Later, should there be a critical problem obviously more threatening to efficient operations, the original casual exposures to the police chaplain pay off. Lines of communication have been opened. Counseling is expedited. Scratch a few more negative statistics.

This matter of counseling in police-community relations is given top priority in Cincinnati, Ohio, where there is an active Police-Clergy Crisis Counseling Program that started in July, 1971. I quote two of the purposes from the training memo:

- To assure the utilization of District Chaplains in situations calling for their services.
- To provide procedure enabling police officers to refer certain non-emergency cases directly to the Police-Clergy Crisis Counseling Team for follow-up investigation and disposition.

For administrators interested in how this is implemented in the field, here is Cincinnati's procedure:

> "When a police officer is involved in a crisis situation and he believes that the presence of a District Chaplain will assist in a proper resolution of the problem or task at hand, he will so notify his district station. The desk man on duty will phone the District Chief Chaplain, or an alternate Chaplain in his absence, and request assistance. Information conveyed should include the nature of the situation, name of the person or persons involved, and the location where the District Chaplain is to respond.
>
> 1. District Chaplains who respond to a request for assistance or provide a police-clergy counseling service will report details in triplicate on the Cincinnati Police Division Chaplain Report.
>
>   a. Original to District Commander,
>   b. First copy to Community Relations Bureau,
>   c. Second copy to Chief Chaplain.
>
> 2. Normally, officers should not request the response of a District Chaplain representing a specific religious denomination to an emergency crisis counseling situation; however, if the crisis at hand would be best served, and time will permit, every effort will be made to fulfill the request."

Just about everybody has seen "Hawaii Five-O." I've been in six sequences of this top television show, so many have seen me on their TV screen. No, you did not see me as the chaplain of Waikiki Beach or a chaplain with the Honolulu Police Department.

I played such diverse roles as a mod young newscaster for a rock-and-roll station, an assistant district attorney who gets himself assassinated, a Roman Catholic priest who is murdered, a tourist arrested for receiving stolen property and a hit man for a local crime syndicate who is killed in an inner-gang knifing. In a way, these violent roles keep me on my toes in my work as a police chaplain. I see these allied types. I know better how they feel for having acted out their roles myself.

Viewers of "Hawaii Five-O" know that the police either use a standard blue-and-white car, recognizable as a police car, or other colors and types of cars recognizable only by the blue roof light. Actually, the latter are more common because the Honolulu policemen supply their own cars. This is easy on a tight city and county budget, but it also has the dividend that off-duty cops in their own cars are never really off duty. In emergencies they are immediately aware through police radio, and available to swing into action.

Each officer receives a monthly allowance toward his finance payments, a portion of the auto insurance premium, and reimbursement of gas and oil costs. Besides the detachable blue light and police radio, all that is supplied is police emergency equipment stored in the trunk.

These cars are something else again. Picture yourself getting overtaken by the charging sound of a high-performance engine as a crimson red Oldsmobile 4-4-2 speed shifts into third gear, passes and wails out of sight ahead of you. A hot-rodder? No, a cop.

Captain Eugene Ouemara's '69 Chevelle SS is a sight to see. The engine has chrome headers and 396 cubes of power. It is not unusual to see a Cutlass Supreme or Grand Prix in the 6000 dollars and up price brackets. Some less flashy cars are equipped with high-performance engines, heavy-duty automatic transmissions, special suspension, and racing wheels.

Many of the officers were interrogated for operating high-powered ultra-sports models and hot-rods. There is now a movement afoot toward more conservative controls, and it may come to city-supplied police cars and the end of the "rainbow fleet."

But meanwhile every time I get into one of these police cars I can't help but feel a touch of excitement, like when I was a teenage hot-rodder, drag-racing, and making an impression on the "wahines" (girls). It's a feeling of power. Add a badge and a gun and. . . .

You have a picture with a very important element missing.

"For what shall it profit a man, if he shall gain the whole world, and lose his own soul?" (Mark 8:36).

Policemen are busy people. They, perhaps even more than others, can easily forget in their busyness the more important things in life. Immersed in "heavy" things of the world, they can neglect the more subtle essentials of happiness—love of family and love of God.

Enter the police chaplain, a gentle friend and soulful reminder.

CHAPTER FIVE

Police Chaplains In The U.S. Cities

Wherever I travel I check in with the police departments.

Sound ominous? I'm just curious—curious to see if they have police chaplains. If they have, we share mutual problems, experiences, and successes. If they haven't, I plant a seed.

More don't than do. From Bakersfield, California to Bangor, Maine, I find an interest in a police chaplaincy program, but no steps taken to carry that interest forward. Besides visiting countless police departments, I have written to scores more. I am always thrilled to hear of successes. I don't think I have ever come across a case where a police chaplaincy existed and wasn't doing a job that needed to be done.

There have been problems—and I'll go into some in this chapter—but there have been far more solutions.

Interest in how to begin a police chaplaincy is everywhere. And that's good news. Even from North Pole, Alaska, where they have only a three-man police force, Patrolman Richard Hawk sounds that note of interest when he reports no chaplain in the department "as of now."

Bangor has considered initiating a chaplaincy program but it is still in the planning stage. Bakersfield feels such a program could be well accepted and is looking at what other police departments are doing.

In between east and west are such compromises as in Ann Arbor, Michigan, where, when the need arises, they select an officer from the police roster.

And in Omaha, Nebraska the clergy of all faiths cooperate with the police and provide whatever services are needed. "When we need a minister, all we need to do is ask and volunteers are plentiful from all faiths," I was informed.

Now that sounds like a pretty good situation, but "all we need to do is ask" is the key. Does a police department ask for a clergyman when a juvenile is booked for robbery, or when a rapist or victim is interrogated, or when a hooker is picked up? I doubt it. Still, that's when a chaplain's counsel can be one of the most vital ingredients.

David G. Epstein, director of public safety for Iowa City, spent ten years as a military police officer and recalled times when military chaplains went on patrol with him and proved quite valuable. "If Iowa City were a bigger place with more big city problems," he stated, "I am sure we could use a chaplain."

I wish Iowa City growth and prosperity, but no big city problems, and I visualize a police chaplaincy contributing to such problem-free growth.

Some cities and towns have had a police chaplain but, for one reason or another, do not now. A town in Florida had a police chaplain over 25 years ago, but when he got involved in department "politics" the program was discontinued. They have no police chaplain. "But this does not mean we have not needed one," said their chief.

One Indiana city had a departmental chaplain but when he died they never appointed another. Part of the reason for this is that they have their Fraternal Order of Police which appoints a member to serve at special meetings, funerals and other occasions. Also, the sergeant in charge of police-community relations assists bereaved families in every possible way.

Now all this is good. I'm not knocking it. But there is

more that needs to be done. Sometimes it's a budget matter, as in Oklahoma City, where the need is recognized but the way to justify an expenditure is not fully understood.

When I come upon a situation, I recommend contacting the International Conference of Police Chaplains (ICPC) for guidance. (See Appendix I footnote.) So many police departments that I queried by mail have asked me for the name of this organization and for a copy of this book!—so they can move to fill a recognized need.

It's where the need is not recognized that I feel this book has its most important work cut out for it. When a sizable city reports proudly that a minister gives a blessing at their annual banquet, so no police chaplain is necessary, that's when my eyes turn upward! Or that there is a fellowship group, or holiday services—all good, but not really in the same ball park.

Then there are the cities and towns that have already taken the first step and have one or two police chaplains on part-time assignments, voluntary or paid.

Springfield, Missouri does not employ a full-time police chaplain. They already have a volunteer unit functioning as "Police Community Chaplains." These clergymen respond when their assistance is requested and occasionally ride with patrolmen. Since they represent many different religions and react as the situations demand, I say Springfield has the core of a police chaplaincy.

So does Kansas City, Kansas, where several ministers, priests, and nondenominational pastors visit the detention unit regularly on a volunteer rotating basis, mainly to hold Sunday services. A beginning, yes.

It's a better beginning where there is a larger need recognized and at least one man officially designated to fill that broad spiritual need. In Hattiesburg, Mississippi, the Reverend John R. Klem, a Southern Baptist, is a uniformed member of the Hattiesburg Police Department Reserve Division. His responsibility is focused mostly on department personnel and he has led more than one member out of feelings of negativity to a realization of the need for God and for living a Spirit-filled life.

It's a better beginning, too, when a single police chaplain, as in the Little Rock (Arkansas) Police Department, assists staff members and their families with counseling and visits to the hospitalized, etc. Colonel H. P. Abbott, Chaplain (AUS, Retired), reports one case where a suicide was averted and expresses his vision that one day there will be three chaplains, as interest and funds permit, one for each watch.

One Illinois clergyman, where the one-man police chaplaincy is only a few months along, reports that fellow officers still have mixed feelings about it. "Some are apprehensive, some curious, some threatened," he says. He adds, though, that changes for the better take place in these attitudes among those officers with whom he has "on-the-scene" contact.

Whether these one-man police chaplaincies serve smaller cities and towns like Fort Smith, Arkansas, or Huntsville, Alabama, or larger cities like Boston, they seem to have one thing in common: the public goes for the idea. That much good comes from the work is the general consensus, and those with whom the police chaplain comes into contact in the department, in the city government, and in the community easily see its rewarding aspects. Said one such police chaplain, "The public has a different outlook on the department as a whole because of this program."

If support is needed for these fledging chaplaincies, it needs to come from more department higher-ups. Top police officials will find budget-shy city officials loosen up where a solution-oriented proposal such as police chaplaincy expansion is introduced, because they know they will have a solid base of public approval.

A priest who is the one-man chaplaincy in an upstate New York police department theorizes that an educational effort needs to be made in police departments on the thrust of chaplaincies. He feels that too much stress is put on "professionalism" and not enough on how "human values" can contribute to that professionalism and to the higher morale of police officers and their families.

Small one-man police chaplaincies are doing great pioneer work in a field which I feel will expand as its value and continual importance become more widely recognized. Meanwhile they are nurtured in their struggle to survive and grow by those moments when a heart is made lighter or a soul is saved.

A police chaplain in an Indiana city called his most rewarding moment when he was told by a former police chief who had opposed the formation of the chaplaincy that he was an asset to the department. This particular chaplain attributed his now total acceptance within the department to a realization that he is not an interfering outsider but a part of the department making a difficult job easier to handle.

One advantage that a two-member chaplaincy has over the single police chaplain is the addition of denomination. A Catholic chaplain or a Protestant chaplain or a Jewish chaplain, alone, is bound to experience the normal reserve among officers that religious upbringing engenders. Add a second denomination and the "message" is extrapolated to a more ecumenical stature.

This helps with growth as other denominations are then added for greater representation. But what helps most is when the police chaplains are permitted to expand their duties from wakes, funerals, graduations, and banquets to police actions involving crime. When a police chaplain uses talk of God to help disarm a man about to kill his girlfriend, it captures the imagination of force-is-the-only-weapon schools, and a new police-oriented respect emerges.

This also helps to melt away possible opposition from young officers who may not be as dedicated yet as their seniors. And it helps to mellow the administration sometimes frozen into an indecisive position.

As opposition melts and understanding grows, often the duties of the one and two-man chaplaincies are expanded before their number is expanded. They are asked to enter more and more as counselors on matters of welfare, morale, and personal problems of police force members—then of their families; then of other employees of the department . . .

Then they may find themselves asked to take part in training programs, injecting aspects of moral conduct, good citizenship and human relations.

Then they may be invited to ride along to some emergency law enforcement situation. Then to others . . . Then on routine patrols . . .

Then they may even get a part-time salary. Then full-time . . .

And maybe be given a uniform . . .

And possibly even a patrol car . . .

The police chaplaincy flourishes when the activity is found to be rewarding not only to the department and to the community but to the chaplains themselves. Then it is their enthusiasm that radiates to others.

A police chaplain is faced with notifying a family of, first, a brother, then a son, killed in the line of duty. The family is renewed and nourished with his solace.

Another police chaplain talks on gun control and his whole sermon is published in the local newspaper.

"It is rewarding when I see fulfillment of efforts put forth toward keeping families together and rendering an acceptable service in such confidential areas," stated one police chaplain in a three-chaplain department. He added, "It is most challenging when I am called upon to provide a spiritual way of escape from entanglements of individuals who have been caught in questionable snares requiring all the spiritual ingenuity and strategy I can muster for their release."

Most of the modest programs maintain a low profile but, where publicized, invariably get good press. A case in point might be the story written by Bob Lane, staff writer for *The News Tribune* of Tacoma, Washington, which appeared in that paper March 1, 1975. Lane attended a monthly meeting of the six-member Tacoma Police Department Chaplaincy and reported on their discussion of failures and successes with would-be suicides.

Lane first painted a word picture of activities in the police chaplain program. How one may ride for hours in a sergeant's patrol car helping to console an innocent victim of crime or violence. Another may just sit on a bench in the locker room and permit a graying patrolman to unburden his frustrations about how life is passing him by. While still a third, with the police radio turned on in his pastoral study, may be called to a wind-swept bridge to try with words and prayer to persuade a fellow mortal to "cling to life for one more minute, one more day."

But Lane then captured quite definitively the psychology behind suicidal thoughts and how the chaplains have attempted to cope with these crises, and how others in other departments have fared with the same problems, as in the case of a woman who was pulled to safety off a bridge several times but later succeeded in killing herself anyway. Or the officer whose novel approach succeeded: "By the time you hit the ground," he told a banker poised on the ledge of a downtown hotel as he drew his .38, "I'll have three slugs in you." The man climbed back inside.

Press stories help the public to know there is a police chaplaincy program and to understand it. With this understanding comes a more balanced image of the police—no less authoritarian, but much more human.

I have reviewed the small chaplaincies that I have had contact with to give those who wish to see one started in their town or city insight into how to begin. But now let's take a look at some of the more developed police chaplaincies—those that have existed for a number of years, proved their value to the community and grown.

The Reno County Police/Sheriff Chaplaincy of Hutchinson, Kansas, is a case in point. Started in 1968 and now comprising 15 volunteer members from different denominations, the chaplaincy is run as if it were a part of the police department—ministers wear badges and ride in a green car with the traditional gold law enforcement shield, adding the word "Chaplain" printed on its doors. Yet the ministers are not paid and no public funds are allocated to pay the expenses of the chaplaincy. Instead, local busineses and citizens donate between 100 and 200 dollars a month. I don't mention this aspect because it is typical or even desirable, but it does prove that this necessary work may not have to be delayed or its growth stunted until the local legislative solons get the word from their constituency.

Called the "Bible and Badge" chaplaincy, this group is on call 24 hours a day and in constant contact with the law enforcement dispatches. Members, when requested, go to the scenes of traffic accidents, natural catastrophes, family disturbances, suicides or attempted suicides, and other special police incidents. They are called usually when the officer in charge feels there is a need. At the scene they attempt to resolve the immediate problem, with follow-up help offered but seldom sought.

A duty roster is maintained with a minister named each day to be on call the full 24-hour period and at least one other minister named as back-up support. If the person or family ministered to in police actions has a minister, the chaplaincy attempts to make that minister aware of the case.

Other activities include delivering death notices, ministering to county jail prisoners and holding Sunday services at the jail, and helping troubled youth.

Some personal observations about this chaplaincy:

- Emphasis is on direct contact with victims, prisoners, and the public rather than with intradepartmental spiritual matters.

- The police chief and sheriff are said to be in full support of the chaplaincy and treat it as an auxiliary of the Department.

- The chaplaincy is recognized as being able to solve complex problems with the chaplain having a "way" into a situation not available to the "cop."

- Chaplaincy ministers are aware when the spiritual approach does not work and are able to switch easily to the role of friend.

These ministers are doing a fine service to the community and to Christ. People have become Christians. Several lives have been saved. What other criteria are there!

Another great job is being done in Albuquerque, New Mexico. Here Chaplain Commander John A. Price heads a volunteer group of 27 clergymen representing more than a dozen different denominations. Here again the main service is to victims rather than departmental counseling or special functions; however, the latter is not totally ignored. The thrust is toward traumatic situations that people find themselves in—notification and consolation in cases of natural death, accidental death, suicide, abandonment, domestic quarrels, domestic counseling and other police situations.

Chaplain Commander Price is also treasurer of the International Conference of Police Chaplains which I previously mentioned and which was formed in 1973.

Minneapolis has had a Chaplain Corps as an auxiliary to its police department since 1968. Today there are 45 volunteer ministers representing some 20 denominations. A typical way it operates is seen from this example.

A man calls the Minneapolis police. His wife has left him. She is divorcing him. He is lonely, has a "desperate need" to talk to someone. A squad car arrives. The officer sizes up the situation and calls the chaplain on duty. The chaplain responds in 10 minutes and talks with the man for a couple of hours. Then he phones the man's wife and gets the couple together. Soon they are reconciled and attend marital counseling sessions at a local church.

Each volunteer in the Minneapolis Chaplain Corps is an ordained minister serving an area church or teaching in a seminary. All are Protestant, but the corps has made arrangements with Roman Catholic churches in the vicinity to provide a priest when requested. Each volunteer serves a 24-hour duty period. On his shift he uses a car equipped with a police radio, responding only when called by police. He never serves warrants, acts as informant, makes arrests or in any way becomes associated with police duties. His duties involve non-crime problems such as assistance in an accident, attempted suicides, domestic quarrels, or notification of next of kin.

The corps is run without cost to the taxpayers as it is presently funded by the Greater Minneapolis Association of Evangelicals which represents some 150 local churches. A chaplain might respond to seven or eight calls in the course of a duty day. Since much of this is devoted to counseling, this expertise could be a drain on the city budget if paid for at going rates.

All Chaplain Corps volunteers must be at least 25 years of age. They are given five hours of indoctrination training by police and spend two four-hour shifts riding with officers on patrol duty. They are then ready for the final screening committee which judges their ability to cope with emergencies and unexpected situations. These chaplains are doing a great job in adding warmth to the chilling problems of big city life. They have a deep interest in people, and those very people find great comfort in knowing that somebody cares.

Since I have served on a two-man police chaplaincy in Palm Springs as well as on a larger police chaplaincy for

Honolulu, the fifteenth largest city in the United States, I take special interest in seeing how the small chaplaincies survive and give, and how the larger chaplaincies become more and more accepted by large police departments and the metropolitan community.

It's all moving forward for Him—serving, as He served.

Training of police chaplains is an important step. So is the maintenance of close communications above and beyond the minute-to-minute calls to respond. First, let's take a look at this matter of training.

I have mentioned the Minneapolis procedure. Here is the procedure proposed by the Tacoma, Washington, Police Department.

TACOMA POLICE DEPARTMENT
Proposed Chaplain's Training

1. Crisis Intervention training, jointly sponsored by Volunteer Hospital Chaplains, Police Chaplains and by Crisis Clinic (15 hours).

2. Tacoma Police Department radio instruction (1 hour minimum).

3. Ride-along for familiarization (proposed 8 hours with Youth Guidance; 8 hours with traffic; 24 with patrol).

4. Departmental organization instruction by Crime Prevention Unit.

5. General orientation regarding the role of volunteer Chaplain (1 hour by program coordinator).

6. Back-up responsibility for a minimum of one week.

7. Chaplains must be photographed for ID cards and duty picture. In addition they are to be supplied with business cards and nameplate before being assigned to duty as Chaplain I.

Pastor Dan V. Nolta of the Olympic View Friends Church serves as the coordinator of the Tacoma Volunteer Police Chaplains and has a close working relationship with the Tacoma Police Department Chief Lyle E. Smith. The program is just four years old and has seven chaplains representing, besides Friends: Presbyterian, Church of God, Episcopal, Brethren, Missionary Church and Christian Church.

Said Pastor Nolta, "We began as a ride-along program basically but evolved until now we are on 24 hour a day call. Acceptance in the department among the officers was slow at first but now appears to be solid. Real ministry to the officers themselves is beginning to take place."

I think Tacoma has put together one of the best set of specifications I have seen depicting the role of the volunteer police chaplain. (See Appendix II.)

Tacoma spells out duty procedures in an organized way, including tour of duty assignments, records and reports, radio procedures, mileage reimbursement and guidelines for the chaplain ride-along program. It is good to crystallize these matters in the printed word. Colleagues, staff and the public begin to get a clearer view of the chaplaincy and its purposes. The less well-defined and organized the program, the longer it will take to catch on and grow.

In San Francisco, there is a relatively informal program. There are eight chaplains—three Methodist, two Roman Catholic, and one each Jewish, Episcopal and Greek Orthodox. Each puts in as much time for the Department without pay as his church ministerial duties permit. The thrust is intradepartmental counseling. The Rev. John P. Heavey, Catholic chaplain, stated the corps responds to any action where there is danger to the life of a policeman and much time has been spent providing spiritual reinforcement to widows and children of officers killed in action. Recently Chaplain Heavey was presented with a new badge inscribed "To Superpriest from the Thin Blue Line."

Often chaplaincies get started on their own thin line. One chaplain volunteers to help the police department. That help is accepted. But there is only a thin line of mutual understanding. The volunteer's understanding of help is not exactly the same as that of the police.

In one recent instance, the volunteer's assistance was accepted. He attended police graduation and swearing-in ceremonies, adding his blessing to the proceedings. He provided assistance to the family of an injured officer, and he counseled a young officer and his wife when she was finding it hard to adjust to his rigorous schedule.

But then the chaplain asked for a uniform—and he applied for firearms training. He was refused on the grounds that he was attempting to expand his role into that of a police officer! End of fledgling chaplaincy.

The chaplain's role definitely is important at the outset, otherwise the whole concept can be aborted and set back for months or years. A rough guideline is all that is needed at first. Experience will help to delineate it in more detail to fit the special situations as they arise.

Some of the ways other cities spell out these duties (as have been briefly described on these pages) can be helpful as a starter, but these are flexible. It is far better to fit your own people with a custom job than try to alter someone else's guidelines to fit your people's needs.

Besides the matter of duties and responsibilities, there are the matters of pay or no pay, size of chaplaincy corps, membership requirements, training, administrative procedures, etc. I see wide variances in all of these, but still a job gets done. The spirit is nourished in a milieu where such nourishment is critical.

Take New York City. Here there are seven chaplains representing the major faiths. They are on a paid basis of about 6,000 dollars a year. They are part of a 30,000 member police department. I have seen seven chaplains in a police department serving a population of less than that. Yet New York's millions benefit immensely from the inspired work of these few. Their work is largely within the Department—instructing in morality and ethics at the Police Academy, counseling policemen on probation for dereliction of duty, encouraging and developing religious and fraternal groups within their department, presenting invocations and benedictions at scores of annual department functions, as well as the usual death notifications and funerals.

However, the department still requests them to attend installations, dinners and social functions of some thirty organizations listed as "official" but involving veterans, civilians, and other community members. Is there any time left, even in the seven day a week, 24 hour a day on-call requirements, for a word of succor to the juvenile, or a reminder of Jesus' love to the mugger or the mugged? I doubt it. Funerals in the morning, lectures in the afternoon, visiting hospitals in between, counseling in the evening between meetings and functions—a New York City police chaplain is a busy man for sure.

But I wonder if he is a Jesus cop.

Don't misunderstand. I don't advocate *less* work. I want *more* of it. But so much more that all of the above is handled as routine, passing through it on to the victims where such help is also needed.

Police chaplains can change the atmosphere at an awards dinner just by their presence and certainly by their words. Bravery in action suddenly becomes bravery under God. Move this catalyst out on a street corner where the mob is heating up. Here the chaplain can be a force under God for crime prevention or at least for cooling it.

What I am saying is directed at any city that is requiring

its "thin clerical line" to face only inward to the police organization. Face it outward to the community also! That's where the action is.

I get some measure of support in this concept from the International Conference of Police Chaplains, which is affiliated with the International Conference of Police Associations, in their concise handbook entitled *The Police Chaplain* (see Appendix I). They include among the purposes of a police chaplain program, "to assist police officers *and the people of the community* through a field service ministry." (Author's italics.)

The ICPC also provides for an outreach in their "Duties and Responsibilities," listing:

- Be on call and on the street during any major demonstration in the city or any public function requiring the presence of a large number of police officers.

- Respond to all major disasters in the city: bombings, building collapses, explosions, airplane crashes, multiple fire alarms, and unusual industrial accidents.

I would like to see added:

- Ride with officers on regular tour duties to provide a spiritual word to criminals and their victims *where indicated.*

Certainly the police can benefit from the presence or availability of the chaplain. I don't advocate the watering down of that concept in the least. But the larger police-clergy team concept can be not only watered down but totally eliminated in some police chaplaincies by ignoring direct service to the community at the point of police contact.

Writing on this in *Law & Order* (September 1969), the Reverend John S. Dettleoff of Oswego (N.Y.) stated, "Basically the aim (of the police-clergy team concept) is to have clergymen ride on patrol and work with police officers as the officers perform their regular duties."

The Reverend Dettleoff points out that when the police and the clergy are seen working together it can bridge the communication gap and bring about greater respect in the law enforcement office and his department. "A clergyman often has a peace-making effect on volatile persons and situations," he stated.

And as I reflect on the triggers that were never pulled, the tempers that cooled, and the tears that flowed in my own experiences as a Chaplain, I say to all this, "Amen."

CHAPTER SIX

Generating Spiritual Steam

Speaking at a meeting in Chicago, in July of 1974, Chaplain John Price said about the role of the police chaplain, "He is the man who brings to the lost, the least, and the lonely—the love of God . . . Here is the arena of life. Here people are battered and beaten, questioning the existence of God . . . Here, in the gore and the grime, people cry that God, if He even exists, doesn't care. Here is where the police chaplain lives."

How do you bring the love of God into this "gore and grime"? It is not easy. This is the challenge that faces the Jesus cop. How he meets this challenge is the ultimate measure of success of the police chaplaincy, and the thrust of this chapter.

In the past chapters I have described the differences that characterize police chaplaincies—how one may administer to police, another to those in police custody or to the community, or any combination of these; how some may be a one-man chaplaincies, others with a corps of 20 or more; how some are given a uniform, a badge, a car, a radio, even a salary, while others get none or only some of these benefits; how some require rigid qualifications and training while others need only to be volunteers.

In this chapter, we focus on the one common denominator—God.

Has God a place in this arena marked by "gore and

grime"? Clarence M. Kelley, director of the FBI, thinks so. Speaking before the Festival of Faith in Oklahoma City, in November, 1974, he said, "Sometimes we hear it said that religion cannot mix with daily life . . . (it is) something strictly for private devotions and the inner heart of man. To my mind such a definition is incomplete . . . If religion is to be meaningful, it must be translated into action—helping others and bringing to those in need, comfort, strength and solace."

I agree totally, and I have tried to express my religion this way, whether in the plush banquet hall of a luxury hotel, or the blackness of an alley where horror lurks.

Believe me, it is not easy. It is, in a way, the ultimate test.

But it is not a test of God. It is a test of the Jesus cop.

Recently the International Conference of Police Chaplains adopted a Police Chaplain's Creed:

> "Believing that God is the answer to man's dilemma, the chaplain stands ready to bear witness to the forgiving love and redeeming power of God to all people and especially to those confronted with crisis. He should always seek to be responsive to God's leadership. He should pray that God will guide his thoughts, words, and actions—as his life is made a channel of God's love. His ministry is on behalf of the local community and is truly an ecumenical ministry. He serves as a source of strength to the man and woman of a police agency. He serves as a reconciling force between staff and ranking officers, between police and community."

This really says it. Were I to assume that I could give a modus operandi for other police chaplains' thoughts, words and actions in that gore and grime or in that black alley, I would be standing in God's way.

Each police chaplain must be his own channel for God's

loving guidance when that moment comes. All I can do is tell how He helped me.

Sometimes I just can't talk about Jesus or God. I just am there with the criminal or victim, and listen. On the other hand, sometimes there is a clear-cut invitation. A soul asks for an alternative, then I jump in. I don't think about it, I just jump. Or maybe God pushes me.

The scene was a detention room. The man had been picked up in possession of a fairly large amount of pot. His face was buried in his hands as if he had reached the end of the line.

"There must be another way," he muttered.

"There is."

"Don't give me that Jesus stuff . . . " he growled.

It takes more than that to intimidate me: "Why not?"

"I've heard it before."

"Garbage! You've never *really* heard it, or you wouldn't be here. I'll use different words, if you use different ears."

He looked up, "Go ahead."

We rapped. He interrupted to ask a question or make a comment. But in essence my pitch went something like this.

"Whenever your head is in a bad place it's probably because you're frustrated or confused about something, and then you end up doing freaky things that you can't even explain yourself. That's what sin is all about—doing weird things that we don't already like, and which we usually regret in the long run, but we end up doing them anyway. Right?"

He nodded, started to say something, then changed his mind. He made a motion with his hand as if to say, "You've got the floor."

"God knows that being separated from Him causes hang-ups and ego-trips which make us selfish and unlovable. The final result of these attitudes of ours is fear, aimlessness, discouragement, jealousy, impatience, lust, hate and an exalted feeling of our own importance. These things in turn are responsible for prejudice, war, poverty, the establishment (any phony world system), death, suffering and pain, and every other crummy bummer in the book. God never intended these things to exist in His own universe, and He still doesn't like them."

"So how come He doesn't do anything about it?" asked my friend.

"When man blew it in the beginning, God faced a traumatic issue. What was He going to do with Earth—the rebellious planet—and how was He going to relate to man whom He still loved even though man had kicked dirt in His face?

"What God decided to do for man is the most far-out expression of love that has ever occurred in the history of eternity. God thought up a plan which would make it possible for man to be liberated from his slavery to weirdness and selfishness. But in order for the plan to work, God was going to have to risk His own life.

"The only way man's predicament could be resolved was if God Himself would become a flesh-and-blood human being and live the perfect life that Adam failed to live. If He would blow it just once, the whole solution for man would be shot for good."

My man was now listening in earnest.

"But that's not all God would have to do. On top of all that, He'd have to take the rap for every man's sin as well. It was too late for man to rescue himself, so if it would ever get done only God could do it. The whole responsibility of the penalty for sin which is hell—total separation from God in death—would be the scene God must face in order to save man from being wiped out forever.

"There wasn't a living soul in the whole universe that wasn't uptight about man's predicament, and everyone wondered if God's love could actually be so great as to go to that length to rescue man. To think that God would strip Himself from His sovereign dignity in the universe just to save a bunch of belligerent human beings on planet Earth was a real mind bender, and undoubtedly everyone wanted to see if it could actually happen.

"Well, it did. One night in a small town a baby was born to a poor peasant couple. The circumstances leading up to the birth were rather unusual, but just the same, it happened. Nobody knew what was going on except for just a few obscure people. With hardly anybody realizing what was happening, God had arrived on earth as a human being and all the universe knew that there was going to be a way out for man after all.

"Do you believe that? Do you know that there is a way out for you? Do you realize that Jesus Christ was this person who was born and that He is the only positive answer to your problems you'll ever need?"

Sometimes I get a new light shining from a person's eyes, as I did in this case. Sometimes I get just a shrug. It doesn't matter what you get. You are doing a job that needs to be done, and it can turn a life around.

Another time I was about to leave the beach where I had been patrolling on foot with a beat cop and we were returning to the car when two women ran out of the ladies' rest room at Ala Moana Beach Park shouting, "There's a man in there!"

My buddy and I went quickly over and entered the ladies' room. One of the cubicles was locked and a man's feet were visible through the opening at the bottom of the door.

"This is the police. You are not supposed to be here. Open this door."

There was a pause. Then I heard the latch click. Out came a scared-looking boy of 16 with barely a sign of peach fuzz on his face. We walked him outside, and motioned to the two ladies waiting that it was all right to enter.

"OK. What's the story?" my buddy asked.

The boy's lips were white and tight.

My buddy looked at me. It was the invitation I was waiting for.

"My name's Bob Turnbull. I'm a police chaplain. I don't want to embarrass you. We just want to help you."

We sat down on the grass. The policeman strolled a discreet distance away. The boy talked.

"I guess I just wanted to sit on a girl's toilet seat."

"Have you done this often?"

"No. This was the first time."

We did not file charges. We took him home. I recommended to his parents, who could afford to send him to an expensive private school where he was a sophomore, that they have the boy visit a Christian psychologist. They agreed. What could have been a serious crisis in the boy's life became a stepping-stone to his normal development.

No action. No word. Just presence. It can turn a life around.

It was not my presence. I was just the symbol or channel of another Presence.

There was a similar incident I was involved in. There was one beach men's room that the beat officer checked regularly. It was in the Queen's Surf where there was a bar. Also, homosexuals hung around that area. This building has since been demolished.

When I and the beat cop walked into the men's room there was an 18-year-old boy holding three girls at knife point. The girls' ages ranged from 12 to 14. They were in various stages of undress. We learned later the boy had ordered the girls to disrobe or he would cut them up. He had threatened that the first one to open her mouth to scream would get the knife—a real tough kid.

But when he saw us he dropped the knife and started to bawl like a baby. He was a sexual deviate and we had to book him. But the officer with me was kind, not gruff, and I spoke a word or two of understanding. It was probably the first time in his life that people did not put him down, but instead tried to help him. He really responded to that.

Again, no sermon. Just a spiritual, understanding presence. Or Presence. It can turn a life around.

I don't want to give the impression that it is only a police chaplain's presence, or only a police officer's kind attitude that injects an upward lift out of that "gore and grime."

I am not in favor of small talk. I am in favor of "fellowship." Actually, fellowship is a uniquely Christian word meaning something infinitely more real and nourishing and satisfying.

At most modern social functions men and women come together like pinballs—they just bump up against each other and ricochet around the room. Conversation is at a shallow, extraneous level—the atmosphere usually noisy, confused, and often hollow. Life touches life with the barest contact. Nobody gets too involved with anybody. Professional hangers-on make the rounds to be seen. Bored VIPs tolerate the name-droppers and opportunists. WHAT one knows is utterly immaterial . . . WHO one knows is desperately important. Subtle jockeying for proximity to the "right people" is pathetically obvious.

The more formal the occasion, the more superficial and insignificant the relationships, the emptier the atmosphere and the smaller the talk.

An average cocktail party is a distressing scene of modern man's social bankruptcy. Fellowship is at the other end of the spectrum.

Fellowship is men and women coming together like grapes, crushed, with skins of ego broken, the rich, fragrant, exhilarating juices of life mingling in the wine of sharing and understanding and caring and being sensitive and compassionate.

Fellowship is the fusion of personalities in the person and presence of Jesus Christ, declared or undeclared. It isn't generated by zealous promotion or set up by clever organizers. It occurs when people gather in Jesus' name. My clerical collar, or any chaplain's, proclaims that name.

So my presence at a "bust," be it sex pervert or safecracker, involves fellowship. Whether or not I bring up the name of God, or the Bible or our Savior is not all that critical. Still, I do so whenever it seems the right thing to do.

How do you talk to a sex pervert about God? I have been asked that question. Maybe this incident will answer it.

We had a suspected rapist in the detention cell. I talked to him: "You, again, Mike. Thought you were going to go to a shrink and get it under control."

"I tried. He bugged me."

"What now?"

He looked away. "Jesus-I-wish-I-knew," the words rolled out of his mouth.

"That may be your answer"—he gave me a blank, uncomprehending stare—"only you've got to say it differently. You have to say, 'Jesus, I wish I knew.' "

"Oh man, now don't you start."

I said nothing—just looked him in the eyes. He looked at me and spoke, "I didn't mean that and you know it. Chaplain, lay some words on me. Anything you want to say. Really. I've got plenty of time."

I laid some words on him—I rapped about sex.

"Part of God's plan for your life is for you to experience your sex potential. Sex was His idea, by the way, not yours. He made you to be sexual, but He also told us some things about how we can operate the best sexually. God wants you to be fulfilled 'sexually.'

"Every one of us has two parents from whom we receive equal biological, genetic, emotional and psychological inheritance. That makes us 50 percent male and 50 percent female, in a sense—whether we're guys or gals. In fact, all of us produce both male and female hormones in our bodies. But in a normal guy, his male hormones are dominant and override the female hormones. And for the girls, it's just the opposite. Ok?

"Now, the problem is that our society is messed up. We

make guys feel like they've got to have a super-stud, tough, John Wayne image in order to be all male. The feminine aspects of a guy's personality are usually pushed into his subconscious as he grows up.

"We see this happening all over in our uptight culture where fathers place strong authoritative demands for performance on their sons. This throws a guy's real masculinity out of balance. That's because real masculinity results from an internal 'marriage' of one's feminine and masculine components.

"In other words, your feminine characteristics are intuition, emotion, and the capacity to be teachable, artistic, gentle and receptive. Your masculine components are those that make you rational, aggressive, strong, logical, self-assured, analytical and authoritative.

"Now in you guys, God wants your masculine features to be complemented by your feminine traits. That's not being either weak or 'gay'. That's being all male—a whole person. For the girl, the same principle works, only in reverse.

"The guy whose feminine features have been repressed or denied throughout his life is going to experience real sexual frustrations. What he has missed out on internally he'll try to make up for externally—through lust, through rape, and through all kinds of sexual activity.

"So you see, these problems are only a symptom of something that is much deeper. A guy who does not have sexual control is not really masculine. He is a weak slave to his own desires, and his promiscuous or violent behavior only proves it to be true. He has been 'seduced' by his inner feminine desires. In other words, *he's been had.* And no egocentric male digs that scene."

Here I was telling a rapist to his face that he's not all there as a man. You can bet I have his attention. It's time for me to move in with the spiritual clincher:

"Most guys who rape are obsessed with sexual lust. Lust

is not love. One is selfish where the other isn't. What most guys don't realize is that when they are consciously picturing themselves as being sexual conquerors (the pseudo-masculine image), they are really being seduced by their repressed feminine desires. That's not being masculine. That's being weak. In fact, it's being a slave to a 'woman'—the internal repressed female who is begging to be fulfilled.

"The dude who brags about his sex life is only advertising the fact that his feminine traits of intuition, emotion and submission are starving to be fulfilled and that he's really a messed-up guy. In fact, he's just showing how *un*masculine he really is.

"God created man to be receptive to His aggressive love. But man rejected God's love and tripped out on his own. That means that man decided he was going to try to be 'aggressive' rather than 'submissive.' That's what sin is all about. God created us to be complementary to Him. He wanted His Spirit (aggressive: 'masculine') to have intercourse with our spirit (submissive: 'feminine'), so that we would experience a fulfilling oneness together. That's what it means to 'get it together' in God's program.

"Care to know about God's program, Mike?" My tone was now take it or leave it. I nodded for the guard to let me out. To Mike it appeared I was not going to wait for an answer.

As I left he blurted out "OK! OK!" I gave him a smile and walked on. Later, I sent him a Bible tract and a note, "Talk to a minister about this." He did—at a church near his house.

God does not issue any standard operating procedures to His ministers. He works through them at the right time, in the right way.

If I have nothing to say in a certain situation, I would hope it is not the right time, rather than to think I am missing the boat, or that God happens to be busy elsewhere at the moment.

Accept this fact that it is not the right time, be silent and the dignity of your presence speaks for you. This can generate more spiritual steam than a poorly timed or forced "dearly beloved."

Mini-sermons sometimes come pouring out of me when I least expect them. Frequently they are devoted to giving some person a feeling of self-worth. People who get into trouble with the law are very often people who are searching for identity. They need to prove to themselves and others that they are unique individuals—to be reckoned with.

There was a brawl. The cops were called. They busted a few, including one youth with a "Saturday night special," the cheap pistol that is now flooding the crime market. He was only 19. I dropped by to see him. He was a likable, intelligent fellow.

"How'd you get mixed up in this?"

He shook his head, "Beats me." He was sitting on a stool, his head down. He looked up at me, his black eyes glaring. "I'm Filipino, y'know."

"Get off it!" I fairly shouted, "You know that hasn't a thing to do with it. Don't try to put the blame on your mother and father."

"Well, that's probably when it started." He was sullen now. "Dad beat up on Mom and left her. So it was up to me. What chance does a Filipino kid have?"

Identity. Self-worth. I felt that light flashing inside me. Coming up—one mini-sermon:

"Do you believe in God?"

"I haven't been to church in years. Don't know what I believe."

"Can I lay something on you to think about?"

"Sure," he responded instantly, lifting up his drooping head.

"It's tough when a marriage breaks up. Walking the new route doesn't come naturally, but our Lord has made all the provisions necessary for you to live a consistent and fulfilling life. On top of that He promises to take care of all the dirty work, and when you get plugged into what that's all about, things really begin to happen.

"It's important, however, to realize some significant things He has to say about what you're like inside and what it takes to make you into a true person.

"First of all, no matter who you are or what you have amounted to so far, you are intensely important to Him. He is so wrapped up in you that He would be happy to stop His work in the universe and focus His attention on you personally. In fact, whether you realize it or not, He has in a sense already done that. You might not understand what that means entirely at this point, but we're going to take some 'scenes' from God's intermission in the universe and explore a few things He is trying to tell you personally *right now!*"

My young friend was now sitting on the floor, leaning against the concrete, and listening intently. I read his body language as "My back is up against the wall."

"It's also important to understand what you and God have in common before the two of you can make it together. Since you were created in His image, you should know that you have a spirit just like He does. He made you that way so that His Spirit and your spirit could come together and experience 'oneness' and true genuine love.

"Now when you really love somebody you not only want to be close to that person, but you want to be in a sense 'one' with him as well.

"Since God is only interested in making genuine love with us, He gave us a free will so that we could choose voluntarily whether to love Him back or not. Love involves trust. If you really love somebody unselfishly and you know that he or she loves you that way, too, then there is an element of trust and confidence between the two of you. Without that, love is not complete.

"Now that's the kind of love God wants to have with man—a relationship of mutual sharing that involves confidence, trust and perfect oneness. Things get messed up on our side of the picture when man begins to doubt God's love and questions His character. At one point, man chooses to stop responding to God's aggressive love and starts trying to make it on his own, independent of God. That's what the story of Adam is all about. It may look to you as if God was trying to play games with the good and bad fruit routine, but there was an important reason for it. God set up the tree situation so that man could have the opportunity to express his own attitude back to God. Without that opportunity man would have been a puppetlike creature, without any way to express a yes or no response to the One who wanted to love him completely.

"So, my friend, you have a 'Father' in your house. He loves you. He wants your love, too. Give it to Him. Then watch things happen for you."

End of mini-sermon. What does the police chaplain do now? Pass a collection plate? No, just leave. The quicker, the better. Without me there the words have a better chance of percolating through.

As I write, a Jesus cop is, at this moment, somewhere in the country at the scene of a crisis. A man may be threatening to jump from a building ledge. A wounded officer may be fighting for his life in the intensive care unit of a hospital. People may be lying under blankets at the scene of a highway accident. A policeman's wife may be explaining why she wants a divorce. A criminal may have barricaded himself in a building with hostages.

Every crisis is different. Yet every crisis demands God's intensified presence. As the code reads, "Believing that God is the answer to man's problems and needs, the (police) chaplain stands ready to bear witness to the redeeming power of God and His love for all people . . . especially those in crisis."

These are really two separate steps:

1. Stand ready
2. Bear witness

Sometimes the chance, need or opportunity to take step 2 does not arise. The police chaplain lends his presence (stands ready), but does not participate (bear witness). Usually, this is as it should be. But if step 2 is not taken when it could have been taken the police chaplain is only doing half a job. If this happens too frequently then the entire police chaplaincy runs out of spiritual steam.

Writing for the *FBI Law Enforcement Bulletin,* the Reverend R. Joseph Dooley, president of the International Conference of Police Chaplains, makes a few poignant reminders:

"The chaplain must be all things to all he serves. He must be knowledgeable and prudent; uncomplicated to the simple; gregarious to the sociable; lighthearted to the fun loving; and serious to the concerned. He must try to have empathy for the suffering; sympathy for the bereaved; patience with the emotionally disturbed; and charity for all.

"He represents the church to law enforcement; and the church is as wide in the scope of its activities as it is profound in its meaning and significance."

Realizing his being all things in all situations, the police chaplain is less likely to feel he does not belong. He is more likely to be attuned to the right thing to say at the right time. Instead of remaining discreetly on the sidelines, he will be more moved to contribute. This contribution of the Jesus cop in times of crisis or need is what adds spiritual steam to a police chaplaincy. That kind of energy can really make it go.

However, a boiler is needed to contain steam. If a chaplaincy is new, the chaplain will have to tread more cautiously than if it is established. Cooperative relations need to be developed with department officials, the city fathers, and key community people. This is the "boiler" that can then hold a full head of spiritual steam.

In 1971 a small group of policemen met at the Los Angeles Police Academy to participate in Bible study. Their meetings continued and their numbers grew. Soon they had an organization of policemen of all ranks and faiths. They called themselves, "The Fellowship of Christian Policemen." Today there are over 125 active members, and the movement is spreading to other localities.

Members of the fellowship work with the police chaplains. They join in visits to the sick and assist in counseling. But, perhaps even more significant is the presence of Christian law enforcement officers at the scene of crime and crisis.

What adds spiritual steam to a police chaplaincy? A police force that is spiritually oriented.

The fellowship is one answer. For those who would like to pursue this, information can be obtained by writing Jack Kistler, president of the Los Angeles Chapter, P.O. Box 30179, Los Angeles, CA 90030.

The ultimate answer is to stir up more interest in church and God through those members of the police department who seem willing to cooperate. Some may think Bible study too stuffy. But how about picnics, retreats, seminars, rap sessions, potluck dinners?

Can you imagine a community where the police force is unanimously and consistently aware of the presence of God?

As a crook, I'd go elsewhere. As a police chaplain, I would be able to function even better. As a resident, I would be able to breathe easier.

CHAPTER SEVEN

What A Minister Can Expect When He Becomes a Police Chaplain

Police chaplaincies are as different as the police chaplains themselves, multiplied by the differences of the police chiefs, the municipal government, and the community they serve. One chaplaincy may minister to police officers exclusively, another only to prisoners, a third to these two and the community. Frequently the nature of the chaplaincy—where it stands in this spectrum of variations—is determined by how it gets started.

Take San Diego, California. In 1967 and 1968 that city was experiencing trouble in certain localities. There were charges of police brutality and unnecessary violence. The police department initiated a unique action. It asked local ministers to volunteer for a special duty. These volunteers were then screened and the selected ministers were assigned to patrolling lieutenants, riding along with them and permitting their presence to be viewed by the community.

These ministers were able to dispel claims of police misconduct in the troubled communities and, of course, provide a "cooling" influence. Evaluation meetings were held every two months. It became quickly apparent that the volunteer program was eminently successful. Within a year—in June, 1969—the first official police chaplains were sworn into office in San Diego. Three ordained ministers representing Protestant, Catholic and Jewish faiths were selected by a committee of the San Diego Police Officers Association to serve the officers of the Department by providing spiritual guidance, counseling and conducting ceremonies.

Here was a chaplaincy that got started with the ride-along activity, which some police chaplaincies never quite get to. Then the activities expanded into the more standard framework. Incidentally, the ride-along activity later tapered off in San Diego as the specific need for which it was created subsided.

But compare that beginning with another police chaplaincy that got started in a way any community can start their own. I call it the "Cookies for Cops" plan.

Let's say there is a police department with no chaplaincy existing in it, and no particular officer acting as liaison with a church, as is so often the case. So, a way is needed to get a spiritual foot in the door, to make a wedge for the possible introduction of the beginning of a police chaplaincy.

There is a police department and a nearby church with no apparent connection. How is a connection made? Well, the congregation needs to decide, or the church youth group, or the ladies auxiliary, to do something. And that something could be to hold a bake-in.

Cookies, pies and breads are prepared. At a time when the watch changes, which can be found out by just asking a policeman, a few cars drive to the police station unannounced and unload the goodies. The church minister pops in and asks to see the watch commander.

He introduces himself. "I'm Pastor So-and-So from the local church. We are thankful to the police for the protection you provide our church property even though we do not pay taxes. You fellows check us out just like any taxpayer, so our ladies (or youth) have brought your men some home-baked breads and cookies. It's our way of saying thanks."

He then starts distributing the goodies. At first, the policemen may be a little surprised and standoffish, but then when they see that it's not a peace demonstration coming in the door, that it's giveaway day, no questions asked, and when they smell that fresh-baked aroma, the mood quickly changes to one of party-like fun.

Some patrolmen are flustered. They don't know what to do or what to say. They just sit around and look a little silly, maybe balancing a few doughnuts and cakes, but then they snap them up pretty fast.

A couple of weeks later, or a month, the procedure is repeated. There must be no strings attached. I mean it—no strings attached, no gimmick. The police eating the cookies are not to be considered as fish taking the bait. Nor should the church people expect more surveillance of their property as a result of the cookies. This needs to be done as an act of unconditional love. The group does it because it feels the love of God. It is a way of saying thanks—something that can be done which is appreciated by the policemen. When a person stands in the door and hands out the goodies, he does not do it with a condition. Actually human nature being what it is, the guys are going to be more aware of the church when they pass it, but that is not the motive. The motive is sincere gratitude.

The church that I am using as an example actually found that there were immediately more police cruising through the church parking lot, patrol units coming through at 3 A.M. flashing spotlights at doors and windows to make sure everything was OK. It is natural for them to want to feel more involved with this church. Some may not have even known it existed. Some know it's there but it doesn't register.

Now they see the church, recognize it, and naturally want to help it out. However, if the group has baked with this as their goal, then that is the sum total of what they will receive: a half-baked result. On the other hand, if they have baked with love, not thinking of what they will receive, totally unconditionally then God honors their life, and the church's life.

The policemen who receive this kind of benefit with no expectation in return respond in kind: a feeling of love and rapport with the ministry involved, the people involved.

After the second or third visit, the church group should bring along some informal New Testaments, like *Good News for Modern Man.* They just tell the watch commander they have some new New Testaments for those who are interested: "We'll just stick them in the corner over there. The guys can take them if they want to."

Low-keyed. Unobtrusive. They just make them available, without risking embarrassing a policeman by sticking a Bible in his hand. After awhile, when they realize the Good Books are just sitting and are available to take, the Bibles are gradually picked up. Often a policeman will wait until he happens to be alone and then take one.

Now the time may be appropriate to make an approach about the possibility of creating a police chaplaincy.

The pastor, youth director, deacon, or a leading businessman in the community who is a member of that church should go and see the commanding officer or, better yet, the police chief.

He should explain how the cookie program is a pleasure for the church people to participate in, and they would like to take a step further, perhaps getting involved in some way with heightening the morale of the police officers and men by assisting in emergencies or in counseling situations.

After a little dialogue about how this might work and how there is no need to appropriate any funds, the chief may get some ideas of his own. Maybe there are other chaplains who have expressed some similar ideas to him. It's all minimal—no longtime commitments. It is only natural for the police chief not to involve his officers. They may not take to it.

The first step is taken. Maybe it has to do with giving the blessing at the upcoming police banquet. It does not matter. Whenever a church representative is there, he generates ease and understanding. He keeps his promise. He is there. He performs what he said he would. He does not hassle anyone. He's in. The minimal involvement will flourish. A police chaplaincy will begin.

From here it depends on how precise the minister is, presenting a picture of the police chaplaincy. Something in print like *The Police Chaplain's Handbook* prepared by the International Conference of Police Chaplains would be excellent; so would a copy of this book. He needs to shoot high, start from where he is and go one step at a time–but keep pushing for a full police chaplaincy with a complete spectrum of activities.

No expense may be allowed at the start. But any department can afford to arrange a uniform, badge number, ID number, schedules, ride-alongs. These things fit into the chief's language. These are all things he can see and understand. No need to debate about the fruits. He'll see those soon enough.

So there are two extremes. The chaplaincy that gets started because of a community crisis. And the chaplaincy that gets started with a church-sponsored "Cookies for Cops". Hopefully, they will both lead to full-fledged police chaplaincies. But there is no knowing ahead of time just what to expect.

Once the police chaplaincy is underway, this not knowing what to expect expands three-dimensionally. The Jesus cop has a life-style in which the only thing he can expect is the unexpected.

One way to be ready for the unexpected is to be in good physical shape. We are supposed to be balanced people–body, soul, mind and spirit. We need to be versed in matters of the intellect, politics, and morality. The police chaplain needs to have his "act together" as the cliché goes, and needs to be totally balanced–including his physical stamina.

I like to see a guy, as Paul "Bear" Bryant, coach of Alabama, wants his boys, "lean and mean." That means not overweight, so that if the police chaplain has to assist in a chase he won't be lugging excess baggage. He should be able to run two blocks and not be winded. Whatever the police endurance course calls for, the chaplain should go through it. If he is too old to handle it he really should not be a Jesus cop, unless he expects to just counsel in an office situation. To keep in good physical shape I recommend the police chaplain eat a lot of fresh fruits and raw vegetables.

I'm an organic "nut" myself. Organic is when the vegetables have been grown in soil with natural, *not chemical*, fertilizers and not sprayed with pesticides. This is God-created, as opposed to man-created. God put the seed of life not only into fruits but also nuts and seeds. It is also in wheat germ, the part of the God-made wheat that man refines away, and in bran; the part of the God-made rice that man refines away; and in molasses, the part of the God-made sugar that man refines away. All of this refining that goes on with originally natural foods saps the life out of them. So we need to reinforce modern food with vitamins and mineral supplements.

We really louse up what God gave us. We dissolve vitamins in cooking water and toss them down the sink. So, if we can't stick to natural foods, herbs, seeds, nuts, honey, raw fruit, and raw vegetables (raw because of what cooking does through either the water or the high heat), then we need to add concentrated nutrients of vitamins and mineral supplements to the depleted food we eat.

On the police chaplain's physical fitness program should be lots of fresh water—distilled if your local water supply has chlorine, fluoride and other chemicals in it. Dr. Paul C. Bragg *, former colleague of Bernard MacFadden who launched America's physical fitness program and who at 95 works out on the beach at Waikiki daily for hours at a stretch, believes one should drink distilled water most of the

* *The Man Who May Live Forever*, by Robert B. Stone, Simon & Schuster, New York, 1976.

time to avoid not only chemicals now put into water, but materials that dissolve into water from pipe systems.

I run with Paul, lift weights, swim and do calisthenics. He has been a great influence in my life toward total fitness as God wishes.

Some police departments have work-out classes, judo classes, endurance exercises, gunfiring ranges, and other modes of building physical skills and stamina. The police chaplain should avail himself of all these opportunities for physical conditioning.

"Well, I'll never need it. As a chaplain, I won't be involved in any situation like that," someone may believe.

Don't count on it, my friend. You just never know.

If an emergency situation arises, at least the Chaplain is prepared. The cost of that preparation is a few hours a week for which God promises to repay him with a few years of added longevity, as statistics will show.

So much for physical trials that can be expected.

Now trials of the spirit. And the police chaplain might as well face it. He can expect plenty of those kinds of trials. How does he ready himself for them?

I will share what I do, but here the Chaplain is on his own.

I have a daily walk with our Lord.

When a police chaplain has a "right" relationship with our Lord, when he is consistently dwelling upon the Lord, then, whatever hits him he can handle.

The Bible says, "Greater is He that is in you than he that is in the world." I understand this to mean God's power in us. If He is the King and we are His kids, His power is far greater than anything the world can crank up.

Another verse says, "We walk by faith, not by sight." So if our sight sees certain situations, our response is the Lord's response, providing we are in the mental habit of dwelling on Him in our thoughts. We act instead of react.

The best way to be ready for any trial of the spirit,

hassle or temptation, is to have an ongoing, solid, working, flexible, alive relationship with our Lord Jesus Christ. This draws to us the spiritual energy we need to handle anything that arises in a police chaplaincy. If all the chaplains in a police chaplaincy have this spiritual outpouring of energy through them, then each helps the other and the chaplaincy team can really make spiritual mileage.

When we deal with the public, this spiritual energy can turn into a different kind of energy that God wants to provide to somebody through us. We find that we sense when a man is thirsty and we will give him water. If he is starving, we will know and we will feed him in the midst of no matter what turmoil.

We might administer first aid or provide comfort, transportation, counsel, or a flashlight for somebody who can't find his lost keys. It will be exactly what is needed at the moment. It is not the kind of timely need that a Sunday sermon often meets, or a prayer. Still it is spiritual need being met—God's answer to somebody, through you.

I cannot imagine just preaching to somebody and not being attuned to his or her total needs. And so the police chaplain is an attuned person. There is a song, "They will know we are Christians by our love." The love and sensitivity of a Jesus cop should be all encompassing and overflowing.

Police chaplains can minister to people by their actions without saying a word. However, if those ministerings evoke interest, why then, let go with that "word." That makes it the old one-two punch.

If the person is hurting, tend to his physical pain. Then when that person responds to what has been done, give him the ultimate help—the spiritual answer.

I'm occasionally asked, "Do you pray with criminals?" It has happened, but what is prayer actually? It is a conversation between God and one of His kids. In fact, it is only part of that conversation. Prayer is when we speak to God. When God speaks to us, it is called the Bible. Combine the two and we have a two-way conversation with answers and with power.

Sure, I pray on the job. Police chaplains everywhere do. A prayer on the job can be a silent prayer of heart and mind; yet it is the very soul speaking to the Lord.

Praying out loud in the presence of others can sometimes be a disaster, like a private conversation inadvertently going out over a public address system. It can have the reverse effect of what is wanted, turning off the very person or persons we are hoping to turn on to a closer relationship with our Lord.

Prayer on the job is a must. It is talking to the Lord and asking Him to join us in clearing whatever the situation may be. So He is right there with us, assisting. We never know what to expect in this police work. One thing we can count on, though, is God's help whenever needed, just as He can count on ours.

We are walking along in police uniform with our clerical collar. Perhaps we have a badge that says "Police Chaplain." Two youths see us. "Jesus freak!" they call out derisively. Do we make a gesture of rejection? Turn away? How do we react to the unexpected? Turning to our Lord is the uncommon denominator in all such situations. "Howzit," I reply, a meaningless word, but it really socks a barrel of love in their language. And it just popped into my mind.

I was cruising with another officer, when a call came in about an injured baby. It was passed on to us and we were asked to help get the baby to the hospital. We were told an ambulance was already en route but since we were so close to the address we were asked to go to the scene. Injured baby. That is always an urgent gut-type call. So we stepped on the gas and were there in one minute flat.

As we got out of the car we could see the ambulance tearing up, a few blocks behind us. Its siren and our own had attracted a couple of thrill seekers to follow in their cars. Now they were joined by neighbors who poured out of their houses as we rang the doorbell. A hysterical woman motioned us to go around to the side of the house. The ambulance boys followed.

There was her injured "baby," a Persian kitten that had its paw caught in a water spigot. Apparently the kitten had been poking up into it to see where the dripping came from. Now the paw was jammed up in there and he could not pull it out. He mewed loudly, obviously in pain.

Do we throw up our hands? Turn away?

Everybody was mad. It was like someone had turned in a false alarm. But this woman was no prankster. She was really going "bananas"—tears, wringing her hands, cries of "Oh, my poor baby."

The ambulance boys were walking around in circles sputtering, they were so steamed up. The other officer was about ready to tear his hair out, or hers. Then they all looked at me.

"Is this your injured 'baby'?" I asked the lady.

"Yes! Do something, please!"

I motioned to my buddy to kick the pipe as I held the kitten. The trapped paw came right out. I handed the kitten to its "mother." She was all smiles. "Madam, this is not a baby. It's a kitten."

"Oh, I was beside myself," she apologized; "I guess I should have thought it over more carefully and called some animal shelter people, but all I could think of was the police."

Now one of the ambulance men walked over with something and dabbed the paw with it, probably an antiseptic. Everybody relaxed and accepted the situation. The officer went out to the car while I accompanied the woman into the house.

She continued to apologize as I thumbed through her phone book. I wrote the number of the local animal humane society on a piece of paper. "Tack this up near the telephone," I instructed her, "just in case of another emergency."

She seemed so relieved that I had not yelled at her, that she was appreciative of my helpful act and said, "I promise to call that number!"

I left. When I wrote my report of the incident, I mentioned having prepared that paper for placement at her phone. Later, an HPD officer thanked me for having been of constructive help in what otherwise could have been a waste of everybody's time and energy. I appreciated the kind word from officialdom. The event gave me a good feeling.

Good feeling?

I have mentioned the taunts, like "Jesus freak!" But many people who see the identification "Police Chaplain" are themselves "freaked." "Hey, what's the story? How can you be both a policeman and a chaplain?"

I then have a chance to witness in a modest way, acting as public relations man both for the police department and for God. Most people react positively and are impressed. A few respond, "You mean I am paying tax dollars for religious stuff like that?" So then I point up the volunteer nature of it and that wins them over to my side.

Of course, most people never notice this dual role. Or if they do, they remain silent about it. No involvement. Even policemen—a large number on the force will never really get involved with us. It is strange, but human nature being what it is, we are sort of suspect. You would think that people who hear of something that might be helpful would want to give it a try. Instead, so many just stand off.

The police chaplain, unfortunately, must expect this sort of thing and not consider it a personal put-down. It happens to the best. Of course, there are those chaplains who invite it by coming on too strong. They want to convert the world just for starters. They come barging into a police situation as if they were God's personal ambassador. Such a "hot dog" can wind up hamburger meat.

The first person to walk into a police situation should be a police officer, not a police chaplain. There could be exceptions, like a domestic call. But even here it is really the law being enforced and that is a police officer's job.

The police chaplain is not an enforcer. He is supportive of the enforcer.

I like to be on the spot fast. But if I run into a situation where somebody sees red when he sees a clerical collar and starts ranting, raving and swearing, "We don't want no religious guy here," I like to know that when I withdraw politely and go sit in the car, there is an officer of the law still present and in control.

This has happened a few times in my own experiences and that of fellow officers. We expect it occasionally, so we don't react. We act. "Sorry, just here to help," and we politely step out the door, in the spirit of unconditional love.

Then it happens the other way, too, and we have to expect this also. Once in Palm Springs, I was riding along at night with a police officer and a call came in about a prowler. We reached the address and got out with our flashlights playing around. When we reached the back door we could see signs that somebody had been trying to force the door.

We went around and rang the bell and the lady who had made the call cautiously opened the door. She looked quite relieved to see our uniforms. We made our report to her and promised to keep her house and the neighborhood under close surveillance.

"This happened once before," she explained, "so my husband installed an alarm system. I don't activate it when he is away because it would scare me worse than anybody."

As we talked I could see how nervous she was and also that she had noticed my clerical collar. It was cold, but I purposely had zipped down my jacket to expose the collar. Now she seemed to be addressing her remarks to me and ignoring my colleague. When she saw the cross, she gave an audible sigh. She began to use words like "heaven" and "God," expressing her faith. I had helped to reinforce this woman's strength via her religious beliefs.

Sometimes the whole thrust of a police chaplaincy can take an unexpected turn.

When we embark on a "Cookies for Cops" program, we expect a police chaplaincy to begin.

When we become the first police chaplain on a police force, we expect our duties to expand from, say, ceremonial duties to ride-along duties.

But take Los Angeles . . .

In the 1920s, the Sheriff of Los Angeles County decided to inaugurate a chaplaincy program. History is not clear whether the Los Angeles City had a police chaplain at that time. It is known that for some years prior to 1945, a mechanic working in the police motor transport section served as a chaplain by officiating at funerals.

Since Los Angeles County handled Los Angeles City's prisoners as well as the prisoners from a number of other nearby towns within the county, the Sheriff found the need for a chaplain in this area, especially to assist with a rehabilitation program.

At first the Sheriff invited organized churches to provide ministers for prisoner counseling and worship services. Then teams of laymen from various churches joined the activity. Schedules were maintained and formal programs were developed. When, later, the Jail Commission was established, it provided support for a full-time chaplain by soliciting donations. So the first chaplain was appointed to the Los Angeles County jail system in 1926. He was the Reverend Ira King and he eventually served for 17 years.

Today, 11 chaplains serve 31 detention facilities where over 13,000 men, women and youthful offenders are held daily. Several of these chaplains serve in the adult division, responsible for men and women prisoners. Others work in the juvenile division which handles all wards of the Juvenile Court as well as juveniles in the custody of the County Probation Department. There is a rehabilitation division where the chaplains minister to the released prisoner through follow-up visitation when he returns to the community; and a fourth division conducts services, Bible studies and classes for the volunteers themselves.

The success of this program is in no small way responsible for the development of the chaplaincy program of the Los Angeles Police Department, unique in the nation:

The Los Angeles police chaplains are all sworn personnel employed in full-time police work. They have various ranks and serve in their police capacity as well as performing their chaplain duties. Although most of the Los Angeles police chaplains, in the past and currently, have had theological training they are not licensed or ordained ministers, so the service is basically a lay ministry. Where necessary, officers or their families are referred to full-time ministers of cooperating churches.

Actually, the first official chaplain of the Los Angeles Police Chaplaincy was a full-time ordained minister turned full-time police sergeant. This was in 1960 and his name was Bill Riddle. After being appointed police chaplain, he kept right on as a full-time police sergeant working on vice assignments. On the day of the assassination of Robert Kennedy, Chaplain Riddle was called upon to address the City Council and lead in prayer.

The history of the unique Los Angeles two-pronged chaplaincy program—police department's and sheriff's—has been traced by Los Angeles Police Chaplain Forrest Ralph Evans in a thesis prepared in 1973 in fulfillment of his B.A. degree requirement at Pepperdine University's School of Business.

Chaplain Evans reminds us in his paper of a research project conducted in 1971 by Dr. Robert C. Trojanowics, which reveals the personality profile of policemen. In this chapter in which I have dealt with the unexpected—the only thing we can expect in police chaplaincy work—it is a fitting note on which to end, because the policeman, contrary to popular belief, believes that moral principles come from a power higher than man and that it is important to have faith.

In writing for the May 1972 issue of *Police,* Andrew F. Sikula, Ph.D., confirms this profile by stating that city patrolmen give highest priorities to family security, self-respect, and a world at peace.

The Jesus cop who expects to be the sole spiritual light in a microcosm of gore and grime may be in for a surprise.

The policemen he serves may themselves be dynamos of spiritual energy working with Him for a better world.

CHAPTER EIGHT
The Police Chaplain "On The Street"

The young man was on the edge of his life. He was threatening to jump. He was a marine just back from a war he did not like—Vietnam—and anxious to be reunited with his wife. Instead of finding her, he found a telegram. It explained that she had divorced him and remarried. It was the first he had heard of it.

When I got the call, I asked for as much information as possible on his background. Armed with this, I pushed out near to a ledge where I could talk to him without appearing to be interfering with him physically.

"Tom, my name's Bob Turnbull. I'm a police chaplain. Is there anything I can do?"

He told me the story of the telegram, then said, "I've made up my mind. There is nothing left for me."

"How about the children?" I asked.

"I don't have any children."

"Before you went into the marines, you worked with deaf children. Remember?"

"I remember. Nice kids. But no relation."

"Relation or not. They still remember you. They would like to see you again."

The tactic worked. He began to sob. I talked some more. He talked back. I asked if I could come over to a window closer to the ledge where he crouched. He gave his consent. The conversation continued. Then he reached over for my hand and asked for help.

The fact that was uncovered about working with deaf children probably saved this man's life. It gave him a sense of belonging by reminding him of some positive aspect of his life that had been overshadowed by his marital shock.

The more information a police chaplain has about a responsibility that he is asked to fill, the better he is able to fill it. That applies equally well to the unveiling of a plaque or disarming of a crook.

Let me tell you about Sally, the young hooker. She was being watched by the police and I was around when the vice squad was given the go-ahead to raid Sally's operation.

Timing was important. An undercover officer was stationed on Sally's "beat" to try to get picked up. We kept him under observation. He met Sally and started walking with her to her place. We tailed them. Once he got inside her door we checked our watches. By previous agreement with the undercover man, we waited two minutes. Then we kicked the door in. Both were partially disrobed. She had marked money in her hand.

The cuffs were slapped on her and the wagon called. I asked the police matron if I might ride in the wagon with them, and she agreed. As we got rolling on our way to the station, I introduced myself to Sally. "I'm a police chaplain. can I be of assistance?"

"I'm not impressed with religious people," she said defiantly.

"Do you mind telling me why?"

"Not at all. I'll enjoy it. You're a bunch of phonies."

"Maybe some religious people are phonies. But not all. Just like there are some phonies in your profession. What do you mean specifically by 'phony'? Something must have happened that soured you. I'd like to know what it was."

She looked me right in the eye for a minute to see if I meant it. At that moment I said inwardly, "Lord, make love show through my eyes. Make her see compassion and genuine interest."

I think my eyes showed exactly that, because she began to tell me the story.

It happened about a year ago. She had stopped in a church on her way home from school. She knelt in the back because she needed help. She noticed a youth group at the front of the church, as she prayed. Sally put her head in her hands and sobbed as she let it all "hang loose." As she prayed, the boys in the group had made wise remarks about her busty figure and the girls in the group giggled. Nobody was interested in her problem.

"They were phonies," she repeated as the wagon pulled up to headquarters. "They were all phonies."

I think telling me the story helped her to feel she was being bitter on the whole subject and unjust to sincere religious people. When she was released, I took her to meet some girls who were active in a nearby church. She moved in with one of them. They became the best of friends. She accepted our Lord, changed her profession, and went home to her folks on the mainland.

The information I got in Sally's case came from her own lips. I did not even have to use this information. It contained within its own telling the seeds for solution.

Betty was a stripper. I did not meet her until it was almost too late. She was already in the hospital after attempted suicide in a hotel room, where she was discovered by the maid who called the police. Hers had been a life of luring lecherous men; of six shows a day, seven nights a week; of using live snakes and trained monkeys to satisfy men's demands for sexual vulgarity.

Information saved Betty, too. It was not her information or my information. It came from the Bible.

Up until her hospitalization she shrugged off religion. "When God starts paying the rent," she would say, "I'll listen." But then she picked up a Bible left on her bed and could not stop reading it. She did not want to eat, just read. In two weeks she lost 15 pounds. Her appetite was only for the Word of God. When she got out of the hospital she went to work for a mental health clinic.

Information helps most where there are emotional problems behind the antisocial behavior. You might say that this is universally the case, but where violence or the threat of violence is in the emergency situation, information is not that easy to come by. So we have to walk hand-in-hand with God. That's better than resorting to information to bail us out or the transgressor. It gives the Jesus cop a trusty weapon that all policemen would do well to learn to use.

I'm frequently asked, "Aren't you exposed to danger?" I really have to stop and think about that each time because I never stop to think about it on duty. Guns. Threats. Violence. But am I really in danger? Being a policeman spells danger, but then everybody is in danger. The policeman has an advantage over danger. Danger avoids him.

He's the one whom people call when danger approaches. He can protect them, and himself, from danger. No members of a crime syndicate in their right minds want to "put a hit" on a cop. The whole police department would come down on their heads—heavy, night and day, nothing but harassment and hassling. They want to avoid that kind of trouble. So the word is out—you just don't knock a cop off.

Also, you would not knock a cop off who is a minister. Public indignation would be added to the police indignation. That means double jeopardy for the sucker who takes on a police chaplain—or double safety for the police chaplain, whichever way you want to look at it.

Add our good Lord's special concern for anybody who is upholding righteousness, minister or not, and I would call the police chaplain the safest man in town.

There are always a few who don't get the message. One time in Waikiki, I remember, there were some suspected hit men sitting around a table at a restaurant. It was a sort of crime syndicate meeting. I knew one of them. Let's call him Kemo. They were pointed out to me by a plainclothesman. "Steer clear of that bunch," he warned.

Recognizing Kemo, I impulsively replied, "I'll just say 'aloha.' "

The plainclothesman must have thought I was out of my mind as I turned and walked in. It was not bravado on my part. I felt safe.

I was dressed in my street clothes, an aloha shirt, no uniform. I walked up to their table. I must admit that as I got close and felt their "vibes", I did remind myself of the Lord's powers within me. If God is with me, who can be against me? Then I felt confident, even brazen.

"Good evening, gentlemen," I said jauntily, ignoring their stony "who is he and what does he want" stares. I held up my police chaplain identification. One of them read it aloud. "Hey," I remarked slowly and with a smile, looking him straight in the eye, "It's good to know the syndicate boys can actually read English. There is educated enlightenment amongst the criminal element of Waikiki."

I flashed the ID to the others at the table. "Gentlemen, what you are observing is the word 'chaplain' which means minister. That's right. I'm not a police officer, although I am connected with the Honolulu Police Department. I'm one of the police chaplains."

Then turning to one of the more overstuffed members of the group, I said, "Move over, Tubby. Let your friendly neighborhood police chaplain sit down."

Two faces cracked in smile. The others uttered a guttural note of agreement. Two were white-lipped and rather put out by the whole thing. I slid in and sat down.

"Well, how's business?" I asked.

Dead silence.

"Rev.," said one finally, "just like for you. It couldn't be better, right?"

"Right," I replied, smiling. "In our professions we never lack for opportunities, do we?"

The guys who smiled weakly before now grinned broadly. The ones who were glowering now shifted into neutral. All seemed to warm up. We kicked small talk back and forth and then I turned to Kemo.

"Do you have a contract out on anybody, Kemo?" I asked like we were talking about the weather instead of murder. He turned white and as he was sputtering I laughed and patted him on the back. "You know, Kemo, I got a contract on you."

As I said it, I became real serious and I looked him right in the eyes. "My contract on you is that it is God's will that no man or woman ever perish without having Christ as Savior. The contract given to me is called the Great Commission. I have been commissioned to try to reach every person, every soul, everybody for the Lord Jesus Christ.

"So, I know you, Kemo. My contract on you is that I am going to put a hit on you called prayer. There is no way you can defend against it. It really works. I am going to pray for your soul. I am going to pray that you don't become more of an animal; that instead, you become more of the human being that God created you to be. I am going to pray that God does a number on you that you never forget. I am going to pray that you have such heavy cement spiritual shoes that you won't be able to take a step unless God allows it. How's that grab you, Kemo?"

He just looked at me sullenly. "You speak heavy."

"That's right," I replied. "You may walk softly with a big gun. I walk softly and carry a bigger Bible. Think about it."

Then, turning to the others, "Gentlemen, any time I can be of assistance just call me. My number is in the phone book." As I got up, I said, "I bet this is an evening you won't forget."

There were a few "far out" and "right on" remarks.

"I guess you know I know—I'm the safest man on this island. Aloha—see you in Heaven—I hope."

I left them nodding and laughing.

One year later Kemo went to Samoa—I forget whether it was American or Western Samoa—and got involved in an honest-to-goodness job, no front for anything. I heard he got married and pulled out of the whole scene.

My "contract" paid off. It was one of the best rewards I ever received.

Speaking of rewards, that is a factor that occasionally arises probably more for police chaplains than for police or other clergymen. It is advisable to resist any such offers as they short-circuit the true spiritual payments—the ones that the giver needs to give on a different level and we are due to receive, again on a different level.

Of course, a gift of money is always useful and can be turned into the police chaplaincy account. But then the giver is "discharged"; he feels no more obligation to the spiritual lesson or event. I prefer to leave him in debt to the Lord.

There was a hooker I helped once. After being busted several times, she started coming to me for counseling. She was a beautiful girl, attractive figure, certainly in demand by her customers. She responded to the Lord's power.

She came to my office one day and informed me she had made a decision. She had her head squared off, and realized she had been going the animal route. She was in a trap and wanted out. She had decided to leave Honolulu and go back to a new life on the mainland. She was free to do this, as she had no crime syndicate connections.

"I can't leave without thanking you for the help you have been to me," she said earnestly. "You and your staff have spent a lot of time counseling with me. I have no money to give you."

"I don't want any money," I replied, "I have already received the greatest reward seeing the changes that are happening in your life. That's a blessing to me."

"I do want to thank you," she continued, "I want to give you a gift. It would mean a lot to me if you would accept it."

"Fine, I'll be happy to."

With that, she got up, walked to the door, closed it,

then locked it. As she started to take off her dress, I jumped up and grabbed her by the shoulders before she could disrobe.

"Please, Bob, this is all I have to give, the only thing I know how to do well. I'm sure you will enjoy it."

I had to laugh. "Honey, think of what you are asking me to do. Do you think it will help me and my ministry?"

Did you ever see a hooker blush? This one turned beet red. She restored her dress, reached for cigarettes in her bag, and lit one. Her hand was trembling. "I never even thought about it. I was just doing what comes naturally to me to do."

"Yes, I know," I said comfortingly. "We are going to have to do some work on that 'natural' area and maybe lead it into the supernatural."

I opened the door, returned to my chair behind the desk and motioned her to sit back down where she had been sitting before. "I know you meant it as a gift," I assured her, "I thank you for your thoughtfulness. But if I get involved in this area it certainly is not going to help you or me."

Speaking of danger, my voice did not sound normal. I realized my throat was dry. I felt my skin crawling with goose bumps. It was as if somebody had drawn a gun on me.

When a healthy normal male, in the ministry or not, is faced with a well-put-together young lady starting to disrobe willingly to have sexual involvement, it can be a mind-bender.

I really had to call upon the power of the Lord. With His help, she was made aware of her own impulses, and she gained insight into ways of making a new life-style stick. We talked a few minutes and she left. I never saw her again.

Another prostitute, a beautiful Eurasian call girl who worked the Waikiki conventions, crossed my police chaplaincy path. She kept a date in one of the hotel rooms and after she had pocketed the money and disrobed she realized her client was a sadist. He had her stand up against the wall, spread-eagled, back to him and then he threw lemons at her.

Their splattering against her back gave him his "kicks."

She had no choice but to put up with it and was relieved when he quit, threw her on the bed, and proceeded to satisfy his normal sexual drive. After she split from that room, she was a bundle of nerves. She remembered the card I gave her once. So she came directly to my office.

As we talked I could tell that she was reacting to this event in a positive way. She was glad she was able to talk to a man, me, about that man, him. She saw in me a restoration of her image of man. She saw in me a totally different species of man than the one she had just left. I was to her a godly man. I meant strength to her. She could relate to me as a person, as an authority. I was not one of those super-pious pastors who would never dirty their holy hands by getting involved with such nitty-gritty problems as hers.

I explained the psychology behind sadism and permitted it to lead into a discussion of true love.

"You were created for love. God made you that way. But you will never experience fulfilling love until you find the other half of your real self; somebody who is complementary to you and who makes your existence complete.

"That's why any man who is separated from God will never be content until he comes back to God and has real spiritual intercourse with Him. God designed man so that he would be complementary to His Spirit, and so that the two would fit together in a perfect oneness of love and trust. Man tried to make himself like God (aggressive, rather than submissive). In doing so, He created a God-shaped vacuum which makes him feel empty and lonely.

"Only God is capable of filling that empty space because He is the only one who can fit it properly. Your male sadist will be throwing lemons at a lot of naked backs until he realizes it is a substitute for a need that is much more important within him.

"In a way, what you are doing is just as desperate a plea for love and security. Love of God is the only way. If you want love and security, God says, 'Come and get it, that's what I made you for'." (Revelation 22:17)

Then I summed it up. "God will not let you down. But anything short of Him is going to be a flat-out bummer."

I wish I could tell you that this woman came to be active in the Christian faith; this did not happen, but she did react very positively. She got out of the oldest profession. She married and now has children. Her husband knows her past. They live and work together here in Hawaii.

How I act with suicide attempts, hookers and crime syndicate hit men is me, doing things my way. I don't offer them as standard operating procedures. No way. I act spontaneously as the Lord moves me. There is no other way for me. I don't think a handbook for Chaplain will ever be written giving techniques as is done for police officers. There can be standard law-and-order circumstances but not standard human circumstances. These have to be handled on a moment-by-moment basis.

Of course there are minor categories that can take some generalization. Earlier I spoke about taunting. There could conceivably be standard operating procedures for a police chaplain subjected to derisive taunts. They might read like this:

Taunters and jibers. The greatest disarming factor is a friendly smile. If we show irritation or anger, it just gives them their jollies: either ignore or smile. Also, it is effective to walk up to one of the taunters—they usually seek safety in groups—look him or her in the eyes and speak kindly and directly. It usually takes the wind out of their sails. Proverbs says, "Soft voice turns away anger." The more boisterous they are, the more effective is the soft voice in bringing them down to a level where effective communication can take place.

I rarely get taunts or jibes. More often it is cold indifference. People might stare, or just back off and watch, maybe disdainfully. When I do get some wise-acres they usually throw their taunts and jibes with a drunken slur or drugged craziness. If they are not drunk or on drugs, the taunters usually turn out to have deep psychological problems and might already be in therapy.

Dealing with drunks is strictly a police matter. When they dry out, then the police chaplain can make a contribution. Even though a drunk might be looking and listening and putting on a good show at being sober, he is really not of the mind to reason, talk or communicate. Being high or tipsy is one thing; but really smashed, he is of another world and nothing I do can be of any value. When he finally dries out and shakes off the DTs he probably will not even remember seeing me.

Once sober, he still has a hangover. If the police chaplain can penetrate that, it would be a good time to get to the root of the problem. What was the reason for overdoing it last night? How can that problem be solved? Probing, guiding, always with sensitivity and compassion.

How about the homosexual? What part can the police chaplain play to help toward a solution of such social problems? Usually the homosexual is in the community, not on the police force. I have counseled only two homosexuals, one man and one woman, who were in the police department. It was not easy. I had a difficult time identifying with their problem because I am really into the boy-likes-girl routine.

At the beginning of my chaplaincy work, a trick I learned to use was to mentally translate *him* to *her,* or *her* to *him,* whenever the counseled person referred to a lover of the same sex. Then I was able to become sensitive to their situation merely by translating homosexuality into heterosexuality.

Any homosexual can be helped, as can any gambler, any alcoholic. The only requisite is that he honestly admits his need and sincerely seeks assistance. Then the technique for that help is in getting the homosexual to examine who he is, not what he does. The next step is understanding the tenets of a spiritual life. I put it like this, "If you are a believer and follower of Jesus Christ, you must lead a Christian life in order to have your act together 24 hours a day."

Then homosexuality and maybe some other hang-ups just fall away like an outgrown garment.

The Chaplain talks a certain language to street people; to people in the community; and quite another language to people in the police department. Somehow the manner and intensity with which he says the very same words vary. This stems from a different attitude because of a different level of authority, and different reasons for saying those words.

One moment he may be counseling a rape victim on the street and the next moment a rape victim within the department, like the policeman's daughter about whom I will tell in the next chapter. Same problem, different technique. It seems like a dual standard, but it really is not. The standard in both cases is God's love and compassion coming through, but expressing it comes out differently when it is an external or an internal matter. That is why I am taking the internal techniques and treating them in a separate chapter following this.

Jesus worked in the street. He did not split and hide from the so-called secular. On the contrary, He was immersed in it. His holiness was not reserved for the ivory-tower set or the holier-than-thou clique who bow to each other and turn thumbs down on everyone else. His holiness was for life and living it—it was not for the cooped-up monastery. It was for the sweaty, dusty road. Jesus accused the religionists of emptying God's Word of its meaning by "teaching for doctrines the commandments of men." It was easier for them to obey rules than to love men.

I have met some super-pious Christian pastors who would never dirty their holy hands by getting involved with street ministries. Yet the Holy Word of God says true Christians are "the salt of the earth." Salt works on contact, otherwise it is useless. True Christians are "the light of the world" and light was meant to penetrate darkness, not run from it.

All of which adds up to emphasizing my conviction that the police chaplain has every bit as much work to do on the street as he has within the department, and maybe more. And though everybody including himself may be more comfortable with him tucked away in departmental chaplaincy functions, there's a world of people out there who need him to point the way.

Let me close this chapter with some techniques to clinch a sale—not getting the client to agree to buy, and sign on the dotted line, but getting the criminal to confess and repent.

Take Butch. He was waiting for a hearing when I looked in.

"Butch, you here again?"

"They're always hasslin' me."

"Who did you rip off this time?" I knew. He'd been caught with his car loaded.

"Me? Nobody."

"Did you ever hear the words 'confess' or 'repent'?"

"Confess? I got nothin' to confess."

"Confession opens the door, Butch. Excuses and denials slam the door and bolt it right in God's face."

Butch moved restlessly. Those words have made him uneasy.

"When you confess, God forgives. God's Son, named Jesus Christ, died so that all you need to do is confess. And the door is opened."

"*That* door? Right now?" pointing.

"Not right now, and not that door necessarily. Confess to yourself, and all the doors will be opened. Think about it."

Butch acted as if he did not understand. Later I prayed that he would confess to himself sincerely enough for God to hear.

Make a note of that technique—*prayer.* Very useful. It works both on the street and within the police department.

The next morning I saw Butch again just before his hearing.

"I'm going to plead guilty, Rev."

I shook his hand.

"How about that second word?"

"Waddya mean?"

"Repent. That means being sorry. Not sorry you were caught, sorry you did whatever you confessed. God has been hurt by what you did. When you repent, God forgets His sorrow. You then feel His love."

Butch nodded. Again I think he understood. He pleaded guilty. The judge gave him a light sentence.

What happens to Butch's life now? I really don't know. Suppose you write the end of this story.

While I pray.

CHAPTER NINE

The Police Chaplain Within The Department

How the police chaplain works within the police department can be a whole new ball of wax. It might be compared with how a person acts on the job as opposed to how he acts within his own family.

It can be identical, but then again it can be as different as spontaneity and protocol.

To permit the reader to shift now from the street to the Department, come with me to sit in on a couple of official police chaplain meetings. I did not tape them, nor do I have total recall. But I do have the minutes. The names are changed.

The first meeting took place in January, 1970. We then jump forward a few years so we can get a sense of progress or change. Listen. It's about ready to start.

CALL TO ORDER: The meeting was called to order at 9:10 A.M. by Chief Harold Smith.

The Chief expressed his appreciation to the chaplains who have participated in this program since its inception, and he hopes for the same kind of interest, if not more intensive active participation.

ROLE OF CHAPLAINS: Father Bennett questioned the need for the Chaplaincy Program at present. Chief Smith stated that the chaplains could possibly assist in death cases, traffic and other criminal cases in the area of notifying the next of kin. Reverend Little feels that they will not be able to furnish that kind of service for this large a community.

After a short discussion, it was agreed that there was a definite need for the Chaplaincy Program in the Police Department. Reverend Simpson then stressed the importance of the role of the chaplains. He mentioned that his participation and involvement in this area has improved the police image as far as his congregation is concerned.

Rabbi Goldman commented that the chaplains should reach the cadets and recruits and also police applicants when they are interviewed. Reverend Little stated that he has participated on the interviewing board in the past and feels that this is one area where more of the other chaplains should be involved.

RIDE-ALONG PROGRAM: Chief Smith questioned the feasibility of the Ride-Along Program in which chaplains will ride with sergeants and lieutenants for the purpose of getting to know more police officers. Father Bennett remarked that he found it quite time consuming and difficult to get to know all of the police officers. He feels that this could be a full-time job in itself.

It was suggested that the best time for chaplains to ride with the men on patrol is in the afternoon. Watch commanders should be contacted first so that arrangements can be made. This is an on-going program.

Mr. Charles told the group the area to which he has been assigned and that he will visit these stations to meet and talk to the men when time permits.

Mr. Thomas remarked that he has, in the past, worked quite actively with another police department and used the term, "politely available," without actually forcing himself or his presence on the police officers. He also stated that he has already talked to 51 police officers in the police department here and has sent personal letters to them. This has added a personal touch to his services.

INDIVIDUAL TALENTS: It was brought up by Rabbi Goldman that all chaplains are not effective for different kinds of situations, such as riding with officers, visiting the sick, individual counseling, group counseling, teaching and being involved in recruit training classes. He strongly recommends that we utilize the strong points of each chaplain. Deputy Chief Alfred stated that the chaplains could help greatly with police personnel in the area of ethical considerations.

Officer Baker suggested that the police chaplains meet with wives of the officers also. Police work is difficult, and more so with three different work shifts. This becomes a tremendous burden on the family. To ease these problems, perhaps the chaplains could explain the role of a police officer to the wives, especially wives of recruit officers; civilian employees may be included also. It was suggested that chaplains be invited to the meetings of the 'police officers' wives' auxiliary.

DEDICATION OF HELICOPTER PAD: The Police Department expects to have the dedication of their helicopter pad some time next week. A chaplain will be asked after date and time are known.

MEMORIAL SERVICES: Sergeant Mansfield briefly mentioned that memorial services for police officers will be held during Police Week in May, 1970.

COUNSELING AT THE DETENTION HOME: Mr. Thomas mentioned the possibility of talking with the youngsters at the Detention Home for boys and girls. It was explained that the Detention Home is under the jurisdiction of the Family Court. Such permission, therefore, will have to come from authorities of the Family Court.

ADJOURNMENT: The meeting was adjourned at 10:15 A.M.

The next meeting took place some three years later. A routine had been established. It is no longer necessary for the Chief himself to be present. An officer has been assigned as his liaison:

CALL TO ORDER: The meeting was called to order at 9:30 A.M. by Captain Joseph Thomas.

THE NEW CHAPLAIN'S OFFICE: Captain Thomas briefly reviewed the minutes covering the new Chaplain's Office, administrative notice on the Chaplaincy Corps and the schedule for visits with the Patrol Division.

VISITS WITH PATROL: Reverend Franklin suggested that the chaplains be assigned by sectors rather than on a daily schedule.

The proposed schedule would include their areas of responsibility on a 24-hour/availability basis. Captain Knight asked the chaplains to work this out among themselves and let him know their decision.

A question arose as to cross-denomination conflicts. This would be no problem as referrals could be made to the proper chaplain. The main idea is to stop by and say hello to the men in their districts. At least make it known to the sector sergeants that chaplains are in the area.

HOSPITAL VISITS: Reverend Richards asked whether hospital or house visits could be channeled through the Community Relations Division or through Personnel. He would like to know when departmental personnel are seriously ill or hospitalized. Captain Thomas said he'll work this through the Personnel Division as they would be the first to hear this kind of information.

DISSEMINATION OF INFORMATION THRU THE "BLUE LIGHT": During the past month, Father Bennett reported a total of five calls from officers needing assistance (three calls and two referrals). "It's not much, but then we're only working at this part-time. In many cases, we really cannot help, but officers have said, 'Thanks for just listening to me.' In this way, it is a help to them." Father Bennett feels that since information on the Chaplains appeared just recently in our newsletter, he feels that these calls were received as a result of this article.

POLICE UNIFORMS FOR CHAPLAINS: Reverend Richards explained that at present, his uniform consists of his collar and police uniform and he carries non-lethal weapons. He does not carry a gun.

Reverend Richards said we should look forward to a uniformed chaplaincy for: (1) identification by the public, and (2) creating rapport with the officers. We need a so-called official uniform to serve as some kind of identification. Father Bennett commented that this would serve as an identification when visiting the substations. "We represent the ears in the department—someone these officers can talk to."

TRAINING: Reverend Richards brought up the subject of training to know the department's policies and understand its views. Adequate knowledge of self-defense is important too. Captain Thomas stated, "This again will depend on how much time you people have available to spend with the Chaplaincy Program. As for training with recruits or recall training, you people are more than welcome to attend. Keep in mind that these classes last a week or a month, so be selective."

COMMUNITY RELATIONS: Relative to becoming more involved in community relations work, Reverend Richards feels that the chaplains do have that opportunity. For example, he already has three speaking engagements lined up for this month. Last Sunday, he spoke to a group of high school students on law and order and obedience to fellow citizens. This, he felt, was really satisfying.

POLICE-CHAPLAIN LIAISON: Reverend Richards reported that since Reverend Yasurita has relinquished his responsibility as coordinator of the chaplains, we should be thinking of assigning another chaplain to act as liaison between the chaplains and the department. Captain Thomas replied that he would like to leave this with them to decide. Reverend Richards indicated his willingness to serve in this capacity and wants very much to get involved as he has a lot of free time.

OTHER BUSINESS: The following announcements were made:

1. Identification Tags
   There will be a make-up session this Friday, September 15th, between 8 and 12 P.M. and 1 and 4 P.M. in Room 202. For those of you who have not yet obtained ID cards, you may do so then. As far as dress wear is concerned, regular street clothes are OK.
2. Retirees' Meeting
   A retirees' meeting was held last Thursday evening. This was a meeting to get together with retired police officers to determine what they could do to help the department and what we could do to assist them. There were 44 retirees present and the comments received were great. They really felt as if they were "in" now. Many felt passed aside when they left the department.

ADJOURNMENT: The meeting was adjourned at 10:45 A.M.

Note that these two meetings could have been two months apart for the way the sequence of things progressed. Note also the turnover in police chaplains, with mostly new names appearing.

Establishing itself can be slow work for a police chaplaincy and frustrating work for the police chaplains working toward its growth. Every ministerial function added to the usual routine needs to be cleared through channels. Even routine matters have to be handled in routine ways with routine reports. Of course, all this is a matter of degree. One police department's routine might be termed a lack of routine by some other police department.

A police chaplain in one city may just sit on a bench in a locker room while a graying patrolman unburdens himself about his wife and how life is passing him by. In another city, the police chaplain in the same situation might have to file a report with the personnel director or some other administrator. The graying patrolman who needed to unburden himself might know about this report in triplicate and would, of course, hold back and limit his conversations to small talk.

Or the graying policeman might vent his problem as if it were somebody else's. "Reverend, I know a fellow about my age who . . . "

For instance, I was riding with a sergeant and making notes for my daily report when he turned to me and said, "Bob, my neighbor has a problem with his daughter. She's going steady and she's only 17. They are a fine Christian family and he's worried."

Now I knew he had a daughter 17, too, and that his was a good Christian family. But I went along with his game:

"Most young people go steady not because of love, but for social security. There is a need to be accepted and belong to someone. An advantage of going steady is finding a degree of security. The guy doesn't have to worry about making the big impression on a different girl each weekend. If he dates a lot, going steady is less expensive—less of a hassle. The girl doesn't have to sit by the phone wondering if anybody loves her. She knows that for any social occasion she has someone to be with. This is generalizing but it's nonetheless basic."

"Are there any disadvantages of going steady?" He really asked that one as if it were closer to his home than his neighbors'.

"Yeah—it can stunt a balanced growth of a young guy or gal. Also the disadvantages are that a steady scene tends to be a selfish relationship. 'You're MINE'. That can often lead to jealousy if there is any breach of understanding. Going steady obviously leads to a more familiar relationship. Becoming more familiar, we relax and barriers begin to dissolve. A familiar situation, even for Christians, has too often led to unintentional compromise—a sexual wipeout. Just because you're a Christian doesn't mean your glands have gone out of gear."

I'm sure his next question would have been, "What about premarital sex?" and the one after that, "What can a parent do to cool a situation?" But he looked over at my reports, and then changed the subject.

Back at headquarters I was stopped in the hall. "Bob, we want you to say a few words at the police banquet next month."

"Sure."

Do I begin my talk like this?

"Our whole nation's sick! Sick to death! Literally! And to make matters worse, the country's full of weird quacks pandering their medicine-man remedies.

"Political remedies—economic remedies—social remedies—religious remedies. None of which touches the disease, all of which aggravate the agony.

"There is only one adequate cure—the cross and resurrection of Jesus Christ. Name any of the social diseases that infect our world: war, racism, prejudice, poverty, drug addiction, crime, etc. At the roots of every one of them is good ol' human SIN—a dirty three-letter word. You know what sin is—pride, greed, lust, laziness, selfishness, jealousy, envy, malice, etc. A condition precisely diagnosed by Jesus Christ in Mark 7:20 through 23:

"Evil thoughts of lust, theft, murder, adultery, wanting what belongs to others, wickedness, deceit, lewdness, envy, slander, pride and all other folly—all these vile things come from within; they are what pollute and make one unfit for God.

"The gospel of Christ is the only remedy for that deadly malignancy, and like any medicine, it must be taken to work. If it is rejected, the disease will rage unchecked to its violent destructive consummation—despite the ingenious, frantic answers applied by sophisticated, contemporary man in his lust for relevance."

No way. I'd be out of the police chaplain's uniform with my badge turned in before the cherries jubilee were served. Later in this chapter I'll provide an example of a more temperate, human approach.

Communicating interdepartmentally consumes a great deal of time but it is far from time wasted. The police chaplain needs to touch all the bases.

If there is a job that needs to be done, there may be several people to contact just to clear it. Then we need to do the job. Then we need to get back to those who initiated it to confirm the results as well as write standard reports.

Take a simple thing like a visit to a hospital. An officer in personnel relations informed me that one of the officers in his department was hospitalized with water on the lung.

"Drop in and say hello if you get a chance, Bob."

I did. I stayed about 15 minutes. If I let it go at that, or just wrote the fact in a cold report that the visit was made, I would not be communicating as well as I should.

I write the report but then immediately called the

officer who called me. "I visited the sergeant at the hospital. He's being released tomorrow so I don't think another visit is necessary. I left a New Testament with him, also our new police chaplaincy brochure. He seemed to appreciate my visit."

That phone call was appreciated. It wrapped it up. If we leave something hanging, it's as if we left the phone off the hook. No calls. This way, the personnel officer realizes his call to me was acted upon promptly and that the results of that action became known to him just as promptly.

I can't call honesty a technique, but it surely pays off to be totally honest in police chaplaincy work. I've been almost painfully honest in some cases, and would guess I've been close to being a thorn in the department's side.

An officer came into our police chaplaincy meeting. He was anxious to get in and get out. It was written all over him. He laid his little trip out on us, then got up to split. "Hey," I said, "why don't you stay awhile? If you really want us to be more effective why don't you spend some time with us? If you are not interested in us, how do you expect us to be interested in you?" On a previous occasion when something like this happened and I spoke up, the officer got mad. This one apologized, sat down, and made valuable contributions to the balance of the meeting.

When I say this, it is not for effect, or because "You can't fire me, I'm a volunteer." I say it for honesty's sake. Other fellows speak up too, and it pays off in better communication. We all deal straight with one another and get things accomplished.

Incidentally, that brochure I mentioned had just come out. It is a single folded sheet that is great to hand out to members of the police force instead of a card. It contains a brief statement on what a police chaplain is, then background and availability. It lists a single police department phone number to call, in this case the personnel division, and then it lists all four chaplains by name, church or other religious affiliation, business and home telephone numbers. It is a good technique for reminding the police of the existence of their own chaplaincy.

It is easy to devise standard public relations techniques. But it is a lot more difficult to come up with the right technique for handling one-to-one situations.

Take the time a man walked into my civilian chaplaincy office. He showed me his police identification. He was an officer and pretty high up. He had a problem and I was recommended to him. Could we talk? Of course, I said.

It turned out his daughter had been raped. She had gone out to a movie with a girlfriend in separate cars. They had split after the show. His daughter got back in her car and was driving home when, all of a sudden, a man in the back of the car put a knife to her throat. He threatened to kill her if she cried out, and made her pull over and park. He raped her in the backseat and left. She composed herself and opened the car door just as a police officer drove by. She hailed him and the alarm went out, but nobody had been apprehended yet.

"Reverend Turnbull, I have gone out of my head over this matter. If I could lay my hands on that bastard I'd kill him. Meanwhile, though, I'm short with my daughter—although I believe she did the right thing in not fighting him and risking physical harm—I'm useless to my wife. I'm short-tempered with other officers. In short, I need help."

He was livid about the whole thing. He realized that as a police officer he was responsible to a degree for this episode, and I could see if he ever got his hands on the rapist, in his present state, he would be a one-man vigilante. This would be the opposite of what his procedures should be and his proper attitude as a police officer in the community.

I could see he was full of hate. Fortunately his daughter seemed to have survived the incident, emotionally, and she was not pregnant. The problem was his.

"I'm kind to my daughter but I am so mad about this I am affecting her and my wife. My daughter thinks I'm upset with her—I get so mad even talking about it—I even get mad at God."

We talked at great length. I could not proceed on a straight spiritual line with him. He was not a churchgoer. And now he was not only nonreceptive; he was a minus in the department.

I was not about to make the mistake of saying, "God loves you and He will help you," to somebody who is himself at that moment saying, "God and religion is a bunch of garbage." That's almost humorous. And if the counselor gets a hollow laugh when he makes pat statements, he deserves it.

I let the police officer express his wrath at God.

"I'm sorry you feel that way," I said politely but authoritatively. "I can identify with what you are saying only because it is the exact opposite of how I feel. I have felt the way you feel in the past, though. I've been really ticked off at God."

"You're a minister and you still get mad at God?" He seemed impressed.

"Yes. Because besides being a minister I'm also a human being. In my moments of weakness, I get mad at God. I'll temper my mad with something dumb like, 'Well, God, you might be right' or 'I think you know what you're doing.' It's my slow way of edging out of my position to acquiesce to the truth of the Lord."

I explained to him how I knew this attitude was ridiculous. The Lord is sovereign and all-knowing, but being human we often require time to adjust to God's ways.

He and I became polarized on the hate-God issue, which was part of my strategy, or technique. Then I built a bridge across that difference by my admission that I had occasionally felt that way, too. Now he was listening to what happened to me, which was a step forward. He was asking about what happened that got me to feel that way, how I handled it, and how long it lasted.

The next inference is: *Well, if it swung around for you, maybe it will swing around for me.*

That was as far as we went during the first session. No miracles. He had let off steam. He felt more in control. But if the rapist had been caught at this point in time, this officer would probably still have given him one rough working over.

We met again at his home, where I had a chance to talk to his daughter and reassure her about her father's love, hidden temporarily in his inner turmoil.

We met again at headquarters. At this time I dared to bring up the rapist, because he seemed better able to handle himself.

"That guy must be hurting," I offered. "He's not much of a man to have to do what he did. He's sick in the head, sick in the body. If he was around me instead of wanting to punch him out, I'd think how I could help him."

"Good point," he allowed.

The last time we met was at my office. "I'm reading the Bible. I'm on talking terms with God again." These words were beautiful music to me. He was responding now with love and understanding. He was showing more strength. The last I heard, the family was attending church together again for the first time in years.

The police chaplain has an opportunity to work with members of the department out on the street as well as at headquarters, social functions, or riding along.

Whenever I am on duty or off I walk over to a police officer and say "hello," identify myself and give out my police chaplaincy card or brochure. Sometimes one will get flustered at first, thinking I am an officer checking on him, especially if he is new on the job. In fact, some misread "Chaplain" and see "Captain."

But then I put him straight and at ease. In the minute or so that we chat—and I keep it short to avoid interfering with his work—I try to radiate friendship and warmth. Not: "Remember, God loves you on weekdays, too." More like: "Good to meet you. See you again."

He is triply relieved. One, I'm not a captain, I'm a chaplain. Two, he has a new friend. Three, I've left.

Even the formal duties of a police chaplain within the department do not lend themselves to pompousness, but rather to naturalness.

Call it a technique if you will, but the more formal the gathering, the more I strive to restore personal warmth and genuineness.

At a benediction or invocation, at a graduation banquet or a special police gathering, so many times, a minister will say, "Let's pray," and then read a standard prayer, or use such trite words that they no longer have life to them. Some will use the occasion to get a thought across about somebody or something, such as "Lord, we know this graduating class did not get the highest scores on reward, but with your guidance they will become etc., etc."

When I pray, I pray to the Lord, not to a person. I really get all wrapped up in what I've got to say to Him. But I don't get wrapped up in my own importance. Most people could not care less whether an invocation or benediction is given. So there is no importance to begin with. It is just a formality of Western civilization. If there is a chaplain around it's a good time to make use of him.

Being natural means being honest. So I don't accept instructions as to what terminology to use not to offend members of other faiths.

I was once asked to give an invocation at a convention dinner. "Don't mention Jesus Christ," cautioned the program chairman. "There will be some Jewish people."

"What percentage?" I asked.

"About 10 percent," he replied.

"If there were 10 percent Christians, would you ask a Jewish rabbi to pray in the name of Jesus so as not to offend them?"

So I did what came naturally.

At police banquets when my turn comes, you might hear me say something like this: "Well, it's invocation time and you are all standing up ready for the little spiritual monologue that you won't really listen to and probably couldn't care less about, but you'll put up with it just so you can get on with the meal. Right?"

There might be a ripple of laughter here as people react to unexpected frankness. What you don't hear are the masks cracking as they, hearing my naturalness, become more natural themselves.

"Let's just fool ourselves, surprise God and really take a moment to think about Him. As I say the words, identify with them and say them yourself in your own way, from the bottom of your heart. So we will all talk with God."

Then I begin. And what I say is very conversational. Like it is happening in our own living room. No stereotyped formality. We really get involved. It might be:

"Lord, we are going to have a beautiful meal. What some people won't eat in a month's time we will have today. We appreciate your bounty. We appreciate the warm friendships that we are part of here. We thank you in the name of our Lord, Jesus Christ. Amen."

People appreciate honesty, policemen especially.

CHAPTER TEN
The Future Of The Police Chaplain

The police of our country are the backbone of law and order. Yet, the policeman's image in the community is far from that of the hero it should be. "Lousy cop" is a phrase heard constantly. John Doe will raise Cain when a driver cuts him off in traffic. But when an officer catches him doing the very same thing, the officer is picking on him.

The police are accused of coddling juveniles, but when they catch our kids doing something, the cop is "badge happy."

When force is used on the policeman, we call it "part of the job." When the policeman has to use force, we call it "police brutality."

We complain that something needs to be done about crime; but then, when we can help by testifying, of course we don't want to be involved.

We look down our noses at a policeman speeding on a call, but if the police take more than 30 seconds responding when we call, we gripe . . .

And we continue to gripe about the "lousy cops" as they change a tire for a wife, revive a husband with mouth-to-mouth resuscitation, work overtime looking for a lost daughter, or deliver a child in the back seat of a police car.

Probably the world has never seen so much asked of so few, with so little given in return.

The very least that a community owes to its police force is to provide it with a source of spiritual comfort should members choose to utilize it.

The police chaplain is one small part of the answer.

It is not a substitute for adequate pay. It is not a substitute for a square shake from the community. It is a "shoring up" in the face of these two inadequacies, and in the face of the most trying of all jobs next to that of a military man not only on active duty but in battle.

The police chaplaincy has a secondary advantage of helping to ease these two inadequacies. Where the public has known about the existence of a police chaplaincy, it has always had a positive effect on improving the policeman's image. Improve the policeman's image and you pave the way for a better salary schedule.

Again, I don't want to infer that the police chaplaincy is the total answer. It is one positive step in the right direction that every community should take.

In this final chapter I would like to give some of my views about the ideal police chaplaincy today and how it might look a decade from now.

The ideal police chaplaincy is one in which every member of the police force is a lay minister. There are so many beautiful things happening even where no police chaplaincy exists in a police organization. Police officers who have accepted our Lord into their lives are moved to express Him.

I am kept in touch with the manifestation of this by a newsletter called "The Lord and the Law" published by officers and troopers out of Burlington, Washington.

Here is one story from that publication's issue of May, 1973. It is entitled "Sunday School in a City Jail" and was written by James E. Turner, Chief of Police, Carthage, Missouri:

"In 1968, I was serving as a lieutenant in the Police Department in Carthage, Mo. The Lord spoke to me about the need for a Sunday School class in the city jail. I promised the Lord that I would find someone to teach the class.

"In a short time the Lord reminded me that the need was still there and that no one was teaching the class. Again I promised the Lord that I would enlist a teacher.

"At an altar of prayer in a revival in October of 1970, I said, 'Yes, Lord, I know that I have never found that teacher, but I will get up from the altar and go find someone.'

"I tried to tell the Lord that I just couldn't do it. What would the men who work under me think if I taught a Sunday School class in the city jail? When I rose from the altar, I said, 'Yes, Lord, I will teach the class.'

"I wasn't sure how the chief of police would accept the idea of the class. When I approached him he was very favorable.

"On November 8, 1970, at 9:45 A.M., I held the first class with four prisoners present. My pastor had 500 cards printed for me to hand out inviting people to: 'DOWNTOWN SUNDAY SCHOOL, POLICE LOUNGE, 9:45 A.M. LIEUTENANT JAMES E. TURNER, TEACHER.'

"It wasn't long until the prisoners, plus as many as 14 teenagers and some of their parents, were attending. During the first seven months, five people were converted and one has been called to preach. Many young people attend and are receiving spiritual help.

"A television station in Joplin, Missouri, featured the work of my class on a special program. A year ago I was appointed chief of police here in the city of Carthage. The Lord is continuing to bless His Word as taught in the city jail. I am glad that I said, 'Yes,' to the Lord. Teaching this class has been the greatest experience of my life."

Activities such as this happen all over the country. They go unsung. Where there is a police chaplaincy they happen more frequently. But ideally speaking, with police officers such as Chief Turner, the entire police force all over the country could be expressing this brotherhood and caring as if they were one big chaplaincy.

But it has not come to that. And until it does we need to create more police chaplaincies, further the growth of existing police chaplaincies, and expand the work of police chaplaincies both within the department and as an outreach to the community.

Since I am expressing some personal hopes and views in this chapter, let me begin at the beginning and tell what my preference is for the police chaplain's uniform. I believe it should be almost identical to the standard police department uniform in that community. The only difference should be that the collar should be open, exposing a clerical collar underneath it.

I don't believe the police chaplain should be armed. He might carry Mace, hidden, also a flashlight and a walkie-talkie; optional might be handcuffs, as a back-up for another officer who might need them. We don't want to be completely helpless should the officer we are with be jumped.

Standard department shoes and belt should be worn. The badge should clearly say "Chaplain," and there should be an ID nametag in view stating "Reverend John Doe," and the city police department. The police chaplain should not wear a hat, barehead is preferred, but if a hat is worn it too should bear the badge saying "Police Chaplain."

The main principle to follow, among the many routes to take, in choosing a police chaplain's uniform is that it should clearly show an involvement with the police department, yet with a difference that catches the eye.

Of course, this applies in public. Around the station, the more we get known, the less meticulous we need to be. When we reach that time when all the members of the force know us, we can be as informal around the station as policemen are.

What is inside the police chaplain's uniform is most important.

Warmth is the prime element. Genuine warmth in an outgoing yet quiet, not abrasive, way.

Patience is next. Wow! We really need patience. As I related in the previous chapter, we need to keep nudging, sometimes for years, before common sense steps are taken for greater effectiveness. But it is that way in most bureaucratic situations.

The police chaplain needs to have what is described in 1 Corinthians, chapter 13, verses 4 through 7. Here is mentioned patience. The police chaplain must have patience, not only with the department and its procedures but with the public and with his own colleagues.

He needs wisdom, both that which comes as God's grace and that which comes through learning in direct experiences. He needs understanding; being sensitive to other people's viewpoints; not reacting so much as acting. He needs tolerance. These are the qualities that people respond to even more than to the external garment we call a uniform.

Another quality related to understanding and tolerance is the warm cooperation needed among police chaplains of all faiths. We may have to work closely with Roman Catholics, Jews, Buddhists, Moslems and others.

One of the problems that Christian chaplains face is the belief that Christianity is *the* answer—the only correct answer. I personally believe that myself. But how do we minister to or with people who think that their way is the answer?

We can wind up being polarized. We can become departmentalized within our own police chaplaincy ranks. This can lead to distrust, arguments, abrasiveness, unloving attitudes—all of the nonspiritual qualities. So Satan has a good dirty laugh at the success of his hatchet job!

Who can think highly of a police chaplaincy directed at helping others when its own people cannot even help each other? A police officer who might be a fence sitter on the whole question of a police chaplaincy would have every right in saying, "Those birds can't get it together. They're hassling among themselves. Who needs them?"

Working relationships between police chaplains must transcend ideological differences. They must be close and understanding without compromising their own faith. It may follow for other faiths in their own way, but for me, a Christian, I know the Holy Spirit will make the "arrangements"—interviews, situations, timing, confession of needs. I am guided by the Lord. So I do not have to countenance negatively what the next minister does. I try to remember and express at all times my unconditional love for all.

Pardon what sounds like a sermon. I have a long way to go, but want to share what progress has been made in my own experience.

In New York City, seven police chaplains serve 30,000 members of the police department. An evaluation of their performance showed that they have made a valuable contribution in spiritual and moral guidance. Can you imagine what 100 could do?

There is no way to know what the optimum number of police chaplains should be per 1,000 police or per 100,000 population. It is quite unlikely that such an optimum figure has ever been surpassed and that the law of diminishing returns has been permitted to take effect.

In the ideal police chaplaincy there will be sufficient numbers of qualified clergymen to give assistance and guidance, from recruitment to retirement, to all members of the police force and their families. Policemen will feel free to consult these dedicated clergymen on a confidential basis knowing they have an intimate working knowledge of police problems. And from these consultations, the police will derive the reinforcement and strengthening of moral fiber they need to discharge their duties on a higher and higher professional level.

In the ideal police chaplaincy there will be a complete understanding between police personnel in action and police chaplains on the scene—an understanding by the chaplain of "non-interference" and an understanding by the police of the potential to be received in a situation from "religious intervention."

For example, the police officer rode up on a three-wheeler to a building where a complaint had just been made about a nuisance. As he dismounted, a man was just climbing the exterior stairs to enter his third floor apartment. The police officer shone his flashlight on the man. "Hey, you!"

The man ignored him and unlocked his door.

"Stay right where you are!"

The man turned around.

"Get that blasted light off me, you dirty . . . ! What's your problem?"

"Come down here!" The officer waved. "You're my problem."

I had just been walking by when this happened. It was a total miscarriage of communication.

"Go on inside. It's OK," I called to the man. He was carrying a box which obviously contained a hot pizza pie. He stepped in to his doorway and closed it behind him.

By this time the police officer had turned the light on himself so the man upstairs could see who he was calling a dirty so-and-so. Now he turned the light on me, infuriated. And with every right. I had interfered with a police officer attempting to carry out his duties.

"Who the hell are you?" he shouted.

"Be careful! Do you know me?"

He kept the light shining in my face, searching it, as I approached him.

"Let me see your identification," he ordered.

"Let me see yours," I replied, pulling out my ID.

At this point he was a bit worried, thinking I might be superior in rank to him. When he saw I was a police chaplain, he really got mad. "Where do you come off . . . "

"Wait a minute," I interjected. "Let me tell you what this problem is all about. You've been working a long shift, no relief, and you're tired. You walk into a situation. You don't investigate it. You don't know the facts. You start yelling at the first person you see. This is lousy police procedure. It could have made you look bad. Think it over. You want to talk to that fellow? You know where he lives. But why don't you let him finish his pizza? You know—there's nothing quite so bad as cold pizza."

He listened, and as he cooled off he seemed to really appreciate the fact that I was so sensitive to the situation.

"Twelve hours, man," he confessed, "and just about the worst 12 hours ever. Everything in the book."

He took a second look at the building. All was quiet. He got on his motorcycle, started up, gave me a wave, and roared off.

It could have wound up differently—with charges of unauthorized interference. And he could have made that charge stick.

Another incident:

I passed a Waikiki hotel and saw there was an argument going on between two policemen, obviously recruits, and two military men. It was getting loud and sticky. I walked up to one of the recruits and showed him my badge, "Can I be of help? I don't want to butt in."

He made a be-my-guest gesture. So I walked up to the other recruit who was being preposterously rude to the servicemen.

"Hey, hey," I said walking up to the belligerent cop. "What's happening here?"

We had some polite but terse words. His belligerency toward the servicemen continued. Again I interrupted, "Get your sergeant here."

He called on his walkie-talkie and in a few minutes I was explaining the situation to his superior.

"Do you want to make a formal report?" the sergeant asked me.

"No, I'll leave it with you."

End of incident. End of another case of outright interference by me. I plead guilty.

In the ideal police chaplaincy, there will be no such interference. Police chaplains will understand the jurisdictional division and honor it, even those divisions that are nongeographic, nondelineated, possibly nonexistent. Still, we are not in proper territory unless we have been invited there—a simple guideline to follow, but one that is fraught with apparently mitigating circumstances.

I endorse no compromise here. Law enforcement is police territory, and nobody else's territory—not even a police chaplain's—unless clearly by specific invitation.

The law of our land must be enforced. The alternative is unthinkable. The courts have made this task of enforcement especially difficult recently. The law needs to be enforced with authority, but lovingly. Perhaps the pendulum has swung too far in the latter direction. In their efforts to protect the innocent and grant full constitutional rights to all, the courts have become much more permissive. This permissiveness, often dictated by Supreme Court rulings, has led to law enforcement disasters.

On state and city levels, extreme leniency has given the crime purveyors a new lease on life. The police departments are understandably frustrated in their efforts to do an efficient job. They need interference from us police chaplains like they need another crook given a suspended sentence. What they do need from us is loving support in a job where quick tempers, fractured manners and possibly fractured jaws are just about part of the "job description."

Wanted: *More police chaplains all over the country. But Emily Posts and Casper Milquetoasts need not apply.*

The police chaplain needs to surrender in two ways. First, he needs to surrender his will and his spirit to the Lord—for reproof, correction and love.

Second, he needs to surrender as a servant of the police department, ready to assist in whatever manner requested. Ideally speaking, the police chaplain needs to consider himself last.

But then—as the Bible says—the last shall be first. He who seeks to exalt himself shall be humbled; and the person who is humble shall be exalted.

If sacrifice to others does indeed bring greater strength and love, then police chaplains have a chance to be the strongest, most loved of all people. Meanwhile, their task is to make the policeman the strongest and most loved of all people. When that stage is reached, there will be no need for men of the cloth helping men of the badge and gun. And when the people themselves feel loving and loved there may be no need even for police forces.

Today we can barely see that possibility, it is so distant. Even a small step such as the following can seem "far out":

The watch is changing. The new shift is leaving the locker room. Before the men go to their patrol cars, they stop in the briefing room—it is prayer time. Each in his own way:

"Dear God, protect me and my fellow officers this day. Let there be fewer accidents, fewer injuries, and less sin. Permit Your peace to enter the hearts of the troubled, the suffering and the wretched.

"Give me the strength to apply my authority where needed and the wisdom to use it properly. Let my strength be calm, controlled and statesmanlike.

"May Your love surround my family while I am on this tour of duty, and the family of man, always. Amen."

Direct correspondence regarding this book or speaking engagements to:

The Rev. Bob Turnbull
Waikiki Beach Chaplaincy
P.O. Box 15488
Honolulu, Hawaii 96815

APPENDIX I
Police Chaplain Handbook*

INTRODUCTION

Today, more than ever in the history of the police departments and law enforcement agencies, the need for religious guidance and assistance to police officers is great and demanding.

The Armed Forces of the United States recognized the need for religious and/or spiritual assistance for their personnel almost two hundred years ago when they established the position of "Chaplain." Members of the Armed Forces, as well as police officers, have the need for someone in whom they can confide and for someone who will listen to their problems with empathy. Clergymen, by their very nature and training, are the ideal persons to fill this need.

No man or woman dedicated to the service of our country is continually confronted with more situations that tend to demoralize him or her, and create an emotional, mental or religious burden upon him or her than does the average police officer.

Each day, the police officer is faced with potentially dangerous situations as he comes into contact with the baser elements of mankind. He or she must make split-second

* This Handbook prepared by the International Conference of Police Chaplains, Inc., 1239 Pennsylvania Ave., S.E., Washington, D.C. 20003. Permission to reprint granted.

decisions that are just and right. Many times, the police officer has a need to express his or her frustrations and problems to one who fully understands the circumstances surrounding his or her duties and obligations.

As does the serviceman, the police officer needs to discuss his or her problems at times with someone who fully understands what he or she is up against, yet is detached enough not to be emotionally involved.

Often an officer cannot talk to supervisors or fellow officers about a problem, because they are police officers too, governed by department and agency regulations. He or she does not want to take his or her problems home, because he or she wants to spare his or her family additional worry or alarm.

An officer may not want to approach the department physician or psychiatrist because of these doctors' official positions. His or her own clergyman or religious advisor, although trained in counseling and theology, is not necessarily abreast of the particular problems of a law enforcement officer. In such cases, a police chaplain could listen with empathy, advise calmly, and offer assistance when such assistance is appropriate.

The need for chaplains and their services is a necessary block in the organizational structure of a police department or law enforcement agency.

On call 24 hours a day, the police chaplains stand ready to respond. The key word is "service" and chaplains pride themselves on the fact that they respond any time, day or night, when a police officer is seriously injured or some other incident occurs in the city. "Presence" becomes a very important thing to the chaplain—to be with his men and women whenever and wherever they may need him.

Many law enforcement agencies have no guidelines for their chaplains and members of the force are not aware of the many services that are available from the chaplains. In turn, the chaplains render these services without direction. The

International Conference of Police Chaplains, Inc. (ICPC), which is affiliated with the International Conference of Police Associations (ICPA), recommends that each agency adapt a set of guidelines for the chaplains.

THE CHAPLAIN'S CREED

Believing that God is the answer to man's dilemma, the Chaplain stands ready to bear witness to the forgiving love and redeeming power of God to all people and especially to those confronted with crisis. He should always seek to be responsive to God's leadership. He should pray that God will guide his thoughts, words, and actions—as his life is made a channel of God's love. His ministry is on behalf of the local community and is truly an ecumenical ministry. He serves as a source of strength to the man and woman of a police agency. He serves as a reconciling force between staff and ranking officers, between police and community.

1. PURPOSE

A. The purpose of the Chaplain Program shall be:
   1. To provide spiritual guidance and counseling to all members of the agency or department, both sworn and civilian, and their families in time of need.
      a) The services of the Chaplain are to be available on the basis of need and desire. He is not intended nor does he wish to replace an individual's own clergyman.
   2. To assist Police Officers and the people of the community through a field service ministry.
   3. To provide spiritual guidance, counseling, comfort in times of crisis. The chaplain should be able to put people in contact with the appropriate agency or agencies to help them.

DEFINITIONS

A. CHAPLAINCY: A ministry to the people of a city in the area of field service to and through the police department.

B. SERVICE: The Chaplaincy will provide the services of a chaplain in a radio-dispatched car on a 24-hour, seven-day-a-week basis. At the request of the police dispatcher, the chaplain will seek to bring comfort and consolation to persons involved in accidents, natural catastrophes, or confronted with death.

The chaplain may be called on to assist police officers in a variety of situations including:

a. Death notices—This could be a homicide, suicide, accidental or natural death.
b. Accidents involving serious injury—for comfort to the injured and their families.
c. Persons who are confused or emotionally upset.
d. Attempted or potential suicide victims.
e. Marital quarrels—Chaplain may wish to make appointments for counseling or make referrals as the situation may indicate.

DUTY SHIFT: This depends on the type of chaplaincy. Some departments assign a chaplain for one 24-hour-shift approximately every two weeks. This is contingent on the number of chaplains available. Other agencies have the chaplain on call one day a month. If the department only has one chaplain from a denomination available, he is on-call and expected to respond anytime he is notified by police communications. It is a chaplain's responsibility to arrange for his own substitute if he cannot serve his "duty shift." Schedule could be sent out well in advance so chaplain would know his assigned time.

QUALIFICATIONS FOR APPOINTMENT AS A POLICE CHAPLAIN

A candidate for police chaplain must meet the following minimum qualifications:

Be an ordained or licensed member of the clergy in good standing and endorsed for the chaplaincy by a recognized religious denomination. In some instances a woman religious will be more effective than a man and her services should be obtained.

Show a God-like compassion, understanding and love for his fellow man and relate easily to people.

Maintain high spiritual and moral standards.

Manifest a broad base of experience and professional maturity, emotional stability and personal flexibility.

Be tactful and considerate in his approach to all people regardless of race, creed or religion.

Indicate a willingness to be involved in training that would enhance one's efficiency in meeting and dealing with people in crisis (e.g., trauma intervention). Should be familiar with community medical, psychiatric and other such resources in the local area.

Be willing and available to respond to any and all situations where his presence, as chaplain, is indicated.

Possess a valid and current driver's license.

Never have been convicted of a criminal offense nor

offenses involving moral turpitude. Minor traffic violations are excluded.

NOMINATION AND APPOINTMENT OF A CHAPLAIN

In many instances, a full-time, salaried chaplain is preferable to the part-time volunteer of the past. Working within the agency, the chaplain will get to know the organizational structure, personnel and dynamics more intimately.

Volunteer chaplain programs may be established to give broad spectrum to clergy participation and provide increased availability of community resources. Such a program may be the entire chaplaincy or may be in addition to a full-time chaplaincy.

If the chaplain is to function successfully within a law enforcement agency, it is vital that he be selected with care, and that consideration be given to the particular needs of the department or agency. It would be advisable for the police agency to utilize the services of the local Association of Churches, the Roman Catholic Diocese or Archdiocese, the Rabbinical Council and the Association of Evangelicals.

Chaplains assigned to the police department or law enforcement agency are first nominated by existing religious organizations within the department, upon approval by their ecclesiastical superiors. Should there be no existing religious organization within the department, the department should solicit nominations from the local Association of Evangelicals, Council of Churches, the Roman Catholic Diocese or Archdiocese and the Rabbinical Council.

The Chief of Police, together with the division commanders of the agency, then officially approves the chaplain for an indefinite term, to serve at the pleasure of the Chief of Police and the division commanders.

A chaplain, so approved, is on loan from his denomination. His acceptability as a chaplain is contingent upon his continuance in good standing within the religious organization he represents. The withdrawal of its endorsement of the chaplain brings his immediate separation from duty with the department or agency. The Chief of Police shall be notified of such separation.

Chaplains representing the major faiths in the United States and Canada should be constantly available to give assistance and guidance to all personnel from recruitment through retirement. Their services help provide the moral fiber needed to strengthen police officers in the discharge of their duties. On a confidential basis, police officers are authorized to consult with these dedicated clergymen, who have an intimate knowledge of police problems.

ORIENTATION OF THE POLICE CHAPLAIN

1. *Attend Recruit Training Sessions*

Although a civilian usually is not allowed to go through the entire Recruit Training Program, the International Conference of Police Chaplains recommends that the chaplain be permitted to attend the academy to better familiarize himself with the police officer's role. He should also read the agency's procedural manual, training manuals, the department's general orders, and any other publications put out by the department or agency to acquaint him with current procedures followed by that agency.

2. *Visits to All Divisions*

The police chaplain should make it a point to visit each of the offices of the department or agency from the central administrative headquarters to the outlying divisions or districts. The new chaplain should go to each geographic patrol division and introduce himself to the men and women at roll calls, giving a brief explanation of who he is and what his function will be—placing particular emphasis on the counseling role. In order to keep close to the members of the department, the chaplain should, on a regular basis, visit and talk informally to police officers on the street.

3. Administrative Staff Meetings

He should arrange to sit in on some administrative staff meetings in order to get a working knowledge of high level policy-making, to know in what directions the agency will be going in the future, to have some input to help achieve these goals, and to become a familiar figure to the top management or upper echelon of the agency.

4. Status of the Chaplain in the Chain of Command

By working closely with the top-level administrators of the agency on a day-to-day basis, the police chaplain is in a better position to have his suggestions carefully evaluated and put into practice. He must be willing to take on the widest range of activities and requests for his services. As this process unfolds, he will find his role developing and evolving. He should have access to the decision-makers at all levels of the chain of command.

5. Office Space in a Police Facility

Because of the immediate need for a police officer to consult a chaplain in certain instances, many law enforcement agencies provide office space for the chaplain in some police facility. The INTERNATIONAL CONFERENCE OF POLICE CHAPLAINS, INCORPORATED strongly recommends that all departments, regardless of size, provide the chaplain with an office. The establishment of an office in a central location makes it easier for an "on-duty" officer to consult the chaplain. It not only increases the efficiency and effectiveness of the chaplain; it also makes him readily available for emergency and routine services. Along with the usual office furnishings, the office should have a police radio monitor and the interdepartmental mail service—so that the chaplain could receive all official notices of the department.

6. Ride-Along Program

Another important orientation experience is for the chaplain to be permitted to ride in a police car on patrol. Where it is necessary, the department or agency should authorize the chaplain to ride. This should be done frequently during the initial orientation of a chaplain, and continued as an on-going activity at least once a month in order to keep him in touch with pressures and problems that confront the men and women on the street.

ORGANIZATIONAL STRUCTURE OF THE OFFICE OF THE CHAPLAIN

The police chaplain shall report to the chief of the agency and shall be held responsible for matters pertaining to the operations of the chaplain's office or division. The administrative duties shall include planning, organizing, and directing the activities of the chaplain's division. The chaplain will submit statistical reports on the activity of the office from time to time as deemed necessary by the Chief of Police. Some agencies use standard report forms, which are to be turned in daily. Information of a privileged nature shall NOT be included in the report. Some law enforcement agencies place the office of chaplain under the Community Relations Division; or the Administrative Services; or the Personnel Division. It is up to the agency to decide this question.

The chaplain's division or office shall be staffed by as many clergymen as necessary to accomplish the objectives of the program. Some jurisdictions elect or appoint a board of officers (e.g., president, vice president, secretary, treasurer; or a chaplain commander, deputy commander, and scheduling secretary; or a chairman, vice chairman and secretary). They process new applications; review interim actions taken by individual chaplains; review complaints and receive suggestions to enrich the service. Interim vacancies in the staff will be appointed and confirmed by a vote of the group. Continued failure on the part of a staff member to perform the responsibilities of his position; or to properly represent the chaplaincy will result in his removal from office on a two-thirds majority vote. Staff will meet monthly and/or other times deemed necessary by the chaplain coordinator.

AUTHORITY OF A POLICE CHAPLAIN

The chaplain is not a law enforcement officer, * but a man of God, duly ordained—an approved and experienced representative of his denomination. His responsibility is to assist all officers, upon request, on matters within the chaplain's realm. He shall not in any way interfere with an officer in the performance of his duties.

The chaplains are staff assistants to the Chief of Police. They are authorized to visit the district station houses (precincts) and offices of the agency, and have access to all buildings and scenes where the presence of police officers indicates the requirement or need for their services. The chaplain shall carry on his person the indentification card issued by the department or agency. The chaplain, when on duty, shall properly identify himself, be courteous, and conduct himself in a manner becoming his role and ministry. For this purpose, the chaplain may converse with any member of the department whenever the need for such services arises.

DUTIES AND RESPONSIBILITIES

As part of their official duties with the department, the chaplains are expected to perform the following tasks and other such duties that may be requested of them by the Chief of Police:

* The chaplain may, in some instances, be a sworn police officer or a deputy sheriff with full police powers. (This change was voted and passed at the First Annual Convention, July 1974.)

— Assist department officials in making notifications to families of police officers receiving serious injury or upon death.
— When an officer is seriously injured or killed on duty, respond to the hospital emergency room on request and identify himself to the hospital staff and the hospital chaplain and work with both according to common ethical courtesies.
— Visit sick and injured police personnel at home or in the hospital.
— Attend and participate in funerals of active as well as retired members of the agency or department.
— Be on call and on the street during any major demonstration in the city or any public function requiring the presence of a large number of police officers.
— Counsel officers with personal problems.
— Conduct memorial services.
— Instruct and interview recruits.
— Present formal lectures at the police academy.
— Participate in "in-service" training classes.
— Be willing to enter into training courses to enhance his (her) effectiveness.
— Periodically attend roll calls.
— Attend departmental graduations, promotions, award ceremonies, dinners, social events, etc., and offer invocations and benedictions.
— Represent the department before official bodies upon request.
— Be responsible for the organization and development of the spiritual organizations in the department.
— Public relations efforts.
— Write column for the local police association newspaper, in-house newsletter, or magazine.
— Attend monthly staff meetings of the chaplains and discuss mutual problems and programs.
— Respond to all major disasters in the city: bombings;

building collapses; explosions; airplane crashes; multiple-alarms of fire; unusual industrial accidents and other disasters.

— Provide liaison with other religious leaders in the community.
— Notify as soon as possible the involved person's clergyman in cases of death or serious injury.
— Make proper referrals in unique cases which need specialized attention.

REGULATIONS AND PROCEDURES

The chaplain should have a basic knowledge of the duties of law enforcement officers and seek to keep abreast of new procedures, and be willing to attend training sessions and programs at the academy.

— The chaplain shall conform to all police procedures insofar as applicable.
— He shall be familiar with and conform to radio procedures established by the agency (e.g., the "radio signal" code used by the department). Radio transmissions should be kept to a minimum and directives from the police dispatcher shall be followed promptly. The chaplain on duty should be available to the dispatcher at all times either by radio or telephone. If the chaplain is on vacation or out of town, he will designate a clergyman to act in his absence; and make the proper notification to the communications division.
— Only the authorized chaplain is to drive the chaplain's car. Use seat belt. In procuring gas, use the standard police department procedure. Report any malfunctions or accidents involving the chaplain's car to the proper authorities.
— A chaplain needing to make a long distance call in

regard to a case he is working on should go through proper channels to get the required approval to make such a call. He shall then fill out the proper form so that the department will be aware that the call has been made.

- The chaplain shall not publicly criticize the action of any law enforcement officer, department official, fellow chaplain, or department policy or action. Any chaplain having a grievance will take up the matter through proper official channels.
- The chaplain shall not release any information to the news media or insurance agencies or attorneys regarding cases in which he is involved. All information secured should be held in confidence and used only for the benefit of the person or officers involved.
- As a specialist in the field of religious guidance, he is an advisor to the Chief of Police in all matters pertaining to the moral, spiritual and religious welfare of police personnel.

DEVELOPING THE CHAPLAIN'S ROLE

1. Availability—Part of the Police Team

A chaplain's duties are similar to those of a military chaplain—a man who is always there when the officers and their families need him. Just as a pastor cannot serve his people unless he is one of them, neither can the police chaplain serve the department unless he is part of the police team. He cannot wait for the man and woman to come to him. The chaplain must go to them! He must meet those who need his services wherever they may be—at the station house or in a patrol car; at the scene of a disturbance or disaster; in the hallway or office; or at social functions, as well as their homes.

2. Counseling of Police Officers

Counseling is an important phase of the chaplain's work and, more and more, police officers and their families seek out the chaplain. He provides counseling and consultation for police personnel and families in personal, marital, family, job-related and other problems.

a) Unique Demands

There have been drastic changes in the police service during the last decade. Today, more than ever, the police profession is unique in its demands. According to Clarence M. Kelley, Director of the Federal Bureau of Investigation: "The time has come for Americans to understand and appreciate . . . the humanitarian nature of the law enforcement profession . . . In my more than thirty years in the law enforcement profession, I have known thousands of officers . . . They are human. They have emotions." (FBI LAW ENFORCEMENT BULLETIN, December 1, 1973.)

b) High Stress Occupation

Indeed, police officers are subject to the same kinds of feelings and tensions as other people. Police work is considered a high-stress occupation that involves considerable provocation on a day-to-day basis for the average police officer on the street. The many pressures of the job create an added burden on the officer which may affect his physical, emotional and personal well-being. Police work is an occupation requiring a high level of emotional stability.

Because personal, family or job-related problems are likely to interfere with optimum performance on the job, it is important that counseling services be made available to officers and their families, particularly those with stress-related problems.

In order to adapt to the increased stresses in police work, it is important for officers to have a stable home life. For this reason, more and more law enforcement agencies are setting up FAMILY LIFE SEMINARS for recruits and their wives.

3. Confidentiality–Privileged Communication

The police officer who comes for counseling to the chaplain should clearly understand that this is an "off the record" and privileged communication which will not be reported to officialdom or have any bearing on his or her job-status. This element of confidentiality is very important to the over-all effectiveness of the chaplain and his rapport with the man and woman of the agency.

4. Referral to Other Professional Resources

Because of the demands made on the chaplain's time, the chaplain will most likely be able to offer only a brief, short-term, crisis-oriented type of counseling. If, in his opinion, a long-term counseling program is desirable for a particular officer or family member, he may refer the individual to an appropriate community agency or to a marriage counselor. However, the police chaplain must keep in mind that serious, crisis-oriented problems can arise in a police officer's life and he should be available to offer immediate help with the understanding that other professional help may be recommended when the crisis passes.

5. Two-Way Radio and Emergency Vehicle Status

In an effort to provide a closer relationship between the chaplain and the department or agency, many law enforcement agencies equip their chaplains with two-way radios (for their private automobile) or a car provided by the agency or some charitable source (e.g., an automobile dealer). In either case, the law enforcement agency should be responsible for vehicle and radio maintenance–including fuel and repairs.

Further, insurance coverage for chaplains when on official business should also be provided. Also, there is a growing trend around the country to equip the chaplains' automobiles with siren and red lights to be used in responding to an emergency. In some areas, the Department of Motor Vehicles must declare the chaplain's personal automobile an "official emergency vehicle." Directory of services will be carried by chaplain so that he can make referrals in cases that need special attention. The International Conference of Police Chaplains urges all departments to extend this privilege to their chaplains.

6. Gasoline Allowance

Most police chaplains are supported solely by the congregation which they represent. In most cases, their salary is barely sufficient to sustain the expense of everyday living. All services performed by volunteer chaplains for the department and its personnel, whether emergency or routine, are performed at their own expense. The greatest expense incurred is in the use of their automobiles.

Although some departments may be reluctant to provide transportation for the chaplain, it does appear reasonable that he be given a car allowance. This would help reimburse the chaplain for part of the expense incurred in the daily operation of his personal automobile to perform police services.

The INTERNATIONAL CONFERENCE OF POLICE CHAPLAINS strongly urges departments and agencies to reimburse the chaplain either through some type of mileage allowance or by granting permission to the chaplain to use gasoline supplied by the department for its official vehicles; in other words, to authorize the chaplain to "gas-up" at the department's pumps when he is on official department business.

7. Record of Religious Affiliation

Presently, many law enforcement agencies maintain no

record within the department or agency indicating the religious affiliation of the personnel. This information is of paramount importance when an officer has been seriously injured or has died in the line of duty, so that proper emergency notification by police chaplains and department officials can be made to the next of kin.

The INTERNATIONAL CONFERENCE OF POLICE CHAPLAINS recommends that, at the time a police officer is appointed to the department, a form be completed by the personnel division and forwarded to the chaplain's office. It is further recommended that an officer's religious affiliation be recorded next to his name on the alphabetical list of personnel maintained by each unit of the department. Officers who are reluctant or who refuse to divulge their religious affiliation, would be listed as "no preference." This notation would clearly indicate that the officer had been approached and preferred not to give this information.

8. Public Relations Activities

As a staff person, the chaplain will be necessarily involved in various aspects of public relations. An excellent way to stay in touch with the families of police officers is by writing articles in the department or agency newspaper or magazine, so that the chaplain's service can be explained and topics of interest can be dealt with.

Outside the agency, the chaplain will be invited to give talks and be on a panel of some type, at various schools, churches, business and other community meetings. There may also be interviews on a radio show or television program to discuss some aspects of the chaplain's role in law enforcement. He may be approached about participating in specialized workshops and consulting with other law enforcement agencies.

9. Cooperation with Other Police Chaplains

The police chaplain needs to stay in touch with other chaplains not only in his own area but throughout the country. He should maintain this contact by attending meetings, conferences, and workshops in order to find out what other departments or chaplains are doing.

10. Reading Materials

As in most other professions, reading the literature is a very necessary and important part of learning. In the field of law enforcement, there are a number of books, journals, articles and reports available. The INTERNATIONAL CONFERENCE OF POLICE CHAPLAINS maintains a list of articles and periodicals that can be helpful to chaplains.

APPENDIX II

The Role Of The Volunteer Police Chaplain

I. THE VPC SHOULD BE:

—an ordained clergyman (minister, priest, rabbi);
—trained and experienced in the pastoral ministry;
—trained in crisis intervention by the Crisis Clinic.

II. BASIC ROLE STATEMENT OF THE VPC:

"As part of a team, the VPC is to *assist* the members of the Tacoma Police Department when that Department is called upon to aid citizens in situations involving

—personal and family crises;
—emotional trauma;
—or other pastoral problems and concerns.

III. FURTHER CLARIFICATION OF THE BASIC ROLE OF THE VPC:

—the VPC will at all times be subordinate to and take direction from the police officer in charge;
—the VPC, as part of the team of officers on the scene, will provide his particular pastoral skill in meeting the immediate pastoral need;

—the VPC will remember that his role at all times is that of minister. He is not to play the role of policeman!

IV. TYPES OF SITUATIONS WHERE A VPC CAN BE OF HELP:

—Suicide: attempt and actual.
—Domestic "beefs" (a "defuser" in the situation).
—Delivery of death notices.
—Automobile accidents involving death or injury of any kind.
—Other accident situations involving injuries:
  —home
  —construction site
  —fires
  —drowning
  —other vehicles—train, plane, boat.
—Any community disaster: man-made or natural.
—Juvenile problem situations.
—Pastoral needs of Police Department personnel and personal problems.

V. TO IMPLEMENT THIS PROGRAM EFFECTIVELY, WE NEED:

Communication
—within the Tacoma P.D. concerning the Program;
—among the VPC's;
—between the Tacoma P.D. and the VPCs.

Education
—continued familiarization of VPCs with police procedure;
—acquaintance of police officers with work of the clergy apart from Sunday morning services;
—periodic evaluation of the Program and the sharing of ideas.

Visibility

—Introduction of VPC to all officers on shift.
—VPC "mug shot" posted in the hall.
—VPC to wear his name badge.
—VPC located in place visible to on-duty officers.
—some kind of official ID to display when responding to a call.

Mobility

—VPC must be available to respond to a chaplain's call anywhere in the city;
—ride with the field sergeant;
—ride in a special police car provided for his use;
—ride in his own car with a "walkie-talkie."

VPCs Need to be Called and Used by the Tacoma Police Department.

VI. VALUE OF THE VPC PROGRAM

—It can increase and expand the effectiveness of the Police Department's service to the community.
—It can build greater trust and respect for the Department by the public.
—It can improve the total program of community relations.
—It can help the clergy to grow in their total ministry.